# CHILD
# WEEPS
## IN
# Silence

# CHILD WEEPS IN
## Silence

LOUISE CAMPBELL

# CHILD WEEPS IN SILENCE

*iUniverse books may be ordered through booksellers or by contacting:*

*iUniverse*
*1663 Liberty Drive*
*Bloomington, IN 47403*
*www.iuniverse.com*
*1-800-Authors (1-800-288-4677)*

*ISBN: 978-1-5320-9883-3 (sc)*
*ISBN: 978-1-5320-9884-0 (e)*

*Print information available on the last page.*

*iUniverse rev. date: 04/06/2020*

This book is dedicated to my seven grandchildren—
Christian: bone of my bone, flesh of my
flesh. Your birth gave me joy.
Jordon: adopted, yet dear to my heart.
Timmy: as gentle as the breeze on a spring day.
Shyann: dances as an angel, she is light on her feet.
Owen: Grama's sunshine, you make me smile.
Collen: your smile lights up my day.
Hunter: as delicate as a rose peddle, yet powerful in strength.

and to my children—
Candy, Jamie, Kenny, and their spouses.
my husband Maurice,
and my many friends.

I have counted my many blessings and seen what God has done.

# INTRODUCTION

My mother's name was Dorthy Ainsworth. She attended the Salvation Army Church, where she sang in the choir for two years. She lived in Paris, Ontario from birth until she married my father, Peter Campbell. Her mother was active in fortune-telling. She practiced divination and card reading. She died when my mother was fourteen years of age. My mother's dad was a drunk; she lived at home with him until she married my father.

My dad was born and raised in Barrie, Ontario. The youngest of seven boys, he attended the Presbyterian Church, where his father was a pastor. He was a quiet man who would never raise his voice. His mother stood 4'10". She ruled the house. Although even the smallest of the boys towered over her by fourteen inches, they feared their mother.

My parents met at Brae-Side Camp, in Paris. After two months of dating, they were married. They honeymooned at Niagara Falls, Ontario. It was at this time that they moved to Brantford, Ontario.

After two and a half years of married life, and endless efforts to conceive a child, both of them became desperate. Every one of my dad's brother's had children. Most likely his mother was putting on some pressure as well.

It would have been at this point that a male prostitute was contacted. A date was set. I do not believe my mother would have consented to this; she was frigid with men. I believe she was raped. This would also explain why she held such anger for her husband. All the boys in my dad's family had dark brown hair and blue eyes. To cover up his wicked act, he chose an Italian prostitute. I believe my father was a rebel from the beginning.

That's how I was conceived.

After this time, my mother stopped attending church. She hated the child within her. She wished the baby would die. It is possible that she even tried to kill her unborn child.

By the time I was born; they were living on the Canadian side of Niagara Falls. Mom told me that she had a perfect view of the Horseshoe Falls from her room. She also told me that I was a beautiful baby. I had golden curls and dark blue eyes. She told me the pain all went away after she held me. Sometime after that, when I was two years old, we would have moved back to Brantford.

Everything that I have recalled and recorded in this book has played a role in creating the adult I would become.

# CHAPTER 1

# MY FIRST YEARS

*I* can remember as far back as Saint Paul's Avenue. We were living in Brantford; I was two years old. I remember sitting in a closet. It was dark, and I was afraid. Next to me was an opened umbrella. Through the crack of the door, I could see my mother standing at the ringer washer. I did not like being in there; I wanted to come out. When I told her that, she said I had torn a complete loaf of bread into small bits and that the closet was my timeout.

Our family pet was a black and white Toy Spaniel whose name was Snooksy. I know what you're thinking—how cute. But she was mean, and I was afraid of her. I was sitting in a big comfy chair and she was sitting next to me. She was snapping and growling at me. She had no plans of sharing the chair with me.

I had two favourite aunts. My Aunty Joice was one of them. She made me a jack-o-lantern one year for Halloween. She was always kind to me; she would never have intended to scare me. The jack-o-lantern had an evil, wicked grin. When she came into the house with it, I began to scream. That night in my sleep, I dreamed about the jack-o-lantern. It had wings and was flying. It was screeching as it chased me. I woke up screaming; Mom had to throw it out.

It was Christmas Day. I got a baby doll and stroller for Christmas. I was pushing my baby doll in the stroller. I was in Mom and Dad's bedroom. The colours were pretty in this room. The drapes were in pastel colours—green, peach, and pink. Their bedspread was the same colour as the drapes.

One of my favourite people to visit was my Grama Campbell. I don't remember her well, but I do remember she was pleasant. Once when I was visiting her home, I stood upstairs in the hallway with her. We stood at the window. The sun was shining into the room. It felt warm. This was a nice place to be with my grandmother.

She had a green bowl in her china cabinet. This was my favourite bowl. When we came for dinner, I would ask her for this bowl. She always gave it to me. Dad told me not to bother her for it, but she told him, "If Pattie wants it, she gets it."

At her home, she had a large grand piano. It was made of oak. This piano filled the whole room. There were lots of windows in the room. It was bright and cheerful. The warm sun on my skin made me feel happy. I sneaked into the room, got up on the piano bench, and started to press on the keys. I wanted to make the pretty sounds Grama made when she played the piano.

My dad came storming into the room. He yanked me off the bench and said, "Don't touch it." Grama came in behind him and said, "If Pattie wants to play with it, she can." Dad won that battle. I had to leave

It was in the winter—November, I believe—when my Grama died. I was four years old. I did not fully understand death, but I did know she could not come back. I asked if I could go to the funeral. Mom and Dad agreed that I was old enough. On our way, there was a bad snow storm. The snow was coming down so heavy that Dad could not see the road ahead of him. We ran off the road into a large snow bank. We stayed that night in the home of a kind man and his wife. The man only had stumps for legs. He walked on his stumps; I was fearful of him. I was very emotional that night. We had not left with plans of staying the night. Therefore, we'd brought no bed clothes. I was used to wearing pyjamas that covered my feet, but this time I had to settle for what was available. We went to the funeral the next day.

Neither of my parents believed they would have another child. Then, two years after my birth, Mom conceived again. They named this child Cathy. She was the very image of Dad's mother. Immediately after the birth of Cathy, Mom conceived Sherry. With the birth of two children of my dad's own seed, I became a stench to him.

Dad was stimulated by the most repulsive things. He would often take us on daytrips. On one occasion, we took a trip to Niagara Falls. As children often do, I wandered off on my own. An Italian couple stopped to talk to me. I did not understand their foreign tongue, which frightened me. I started to cry, and ran to Mom and Dad. This gave Dad an incentive to act. After that, he would not let up; he would continually remark on Italian prostitutes. He would say, "Look at Pattie's dark hair and dark blue eyes. She is the Italian prostitute's child; she has no resemblance to the other children." He would be smiling when he said this. He was always talking about it. He did not care whether it was just family at home, or if we had guests. Mom did not like it when he talked about this man. She would tell him to shut up about it. When he talked about it, our guests would stare at me. I did not like it when he did this.

We would often go to Barrie to visit Dad's family. I knew he had also spoken of the Italian prostitute to them. My uncles would watch Cathy as she played. They would say, "She looks like a Campbell. She has our mother's features." They also watched as I played. Then they would say, "She don't look at all like a Campbell. I see no similarity to our family in her." It was different when we went to Uncle John and Aunt Norma's home. They never talked about it. All the time we were there, Aunt Norma would cuddle me in her arms. She would brush my hair behind my ears with her fingers. I never wanted her to stop; it felt good to be cuddled. I was never cuddled at home. She was my other favourite aunt. I now understand she knew everything that was going on.

My Grampa Campbell was a man I did not appreciate enough. Today I realize that he most likely knew of the dirty things Dad was spreading throughout the family. He was a quiet man. I can only recall Grampa speaking to me one time. I can say with much appreciation that he never spoke of the dirty slander. Grampa was a very saintly Christian man. He was truly a person you could look up to.

Grampa's home was not bright and cheerful. The colours—made up of browns, beiges, and cream tones—were very dull. I do remember clearly that he had a big brick fireplace, and on this fireplace was a starfish. I wanted to see it. When I asked Grampa if I could touch it, he brought it down to me; it was a creamy colour. The texture was hard and bumpy. It felt strange. I asked if it had ever been a real fish. Grampa told me, "It was alive at one time, and this starfish lived at the very bottom of the ocean." I found this fascinating. I had to be told to leave it alone, I was so intrigued by it.

At the age of ninety-one, Grampa was in more need of care. He had a catheter, which he was fully dependent on. All seven of his sons sincerely wanted to take him into their home and care for him. For one reason or another, it did not work out for them. The only boys left who could take him in was my dad and my Uncle John. I understand now why he would have been so quiet; he was getting shoved from one home to another. He felt like he was a burden.

One evening we were in the kitchen, and the outside door was open wide. It was a warm summer night. Grampa sat in the open doorway, in a rocking chair. He was rocking the chair in a slow, steady rhythm. Behind Grampa was the kitchen table; on it was a white tablecloth that hung to the floor. I was hiding behind

Grampa, under the table. I felt I was safe from him under there. I was sure that this scary old man would not see me behind the tablecloth. I saw this as my only hope.

Grampa did not speak a word; he was not responding to anything in the room. He just kept rocking back and forth in that chair. He looked so old, the thunder was crashing, and the lightning was lighting up the whole sky. I was horrified. As I hid from him, I was sure he was going to turn around and then something truly scary would happen—like his head would fall off and roll across the floor. I was incapable of being grateful for that sweet smell of the fresh summer rain. Mom had been keeping me up at night to watch horror movies. To me it was like one of those terrible movies was happening inside our own home.

My parents were not cut out for taking care of Grampa. As much as my dad wanted to care for him, neither of my parents were up for the challenge. Mom was not comfortable with the catheter, and Dad quite simply was overworked. So less than two weeks later, Grampa moved in with Uncle John and Aunt Norma. This worked out fine for him, and this was where he stayed until he went to be with Jesus. My aunt was a dear, sweet, and gentle person, so it was not surprising that this arrangement worked out well for them.

One of the most fascinating things I ever saw while growing up was at one of my uncle's home. His wife's parents were midgets. For a four-year-old like me, that was something I never forgot. They were adults who were no taller than myself! My cousins took me down into their grandparents' apartment to meet them. Their refrigerator, stove, and cabinets were the perfect size for a child to play house with. Everything was miniature in size. It did not take long before I had myself thrown out.

My mother's dad, Grampa Ainsworth, was a man I should have been afraid of. But instead, I trusted him. I was totally crazy over him. I believe it was because he behaved like a kid. He was a drunk, but boy could this guy play! Dad came outside and caught him tossing me up into the air. I was full of giggles, and of course he was drunk. This made Dad furious and he started shouting at him. That was when Grampa, in his drunken stupor, decided he was going to get physical. He started coming at Dad with his fist up, ready to fight. Mom must have grabbed me and taken me away to avoid me seeing what was going to happen next.

After my Grampa lifted his fist, I remember no more of this confrontation between them. It would be many years before I would see my Grampa again. I imagine that meant my mom was forbidden from seeing her dad as well. One spouse forbidding the other from connecting with one of their parents has not skipped a generation in my mother's family for a long time. I say this with great pain in my heart. I have been cut off from all communication with my daughter, just as my husband did with me and my mother. I have cried endless nights for my loss.

Today I can feel the pain my grandfather felt. If I ever said his name—Lord forbid I said I missed him—Dad would get angry and start shouting, "*My* father's a good man, that man is a useless drunk."

It was shortly after that Dad bought his first house. Up to this point, he had always rented. He bought a small fifty acre farm in the village of Canning, just outside of Paris. This place was rat-infested. There were holes in the outside walls as big as baseballs. Walking up the steps late at night, the rats would literally run across my feet. At midnight, I could look out my bedroom window and see the rats running in packs, back and forth across the road.

Our farm was divided into two portions of land. On the one side of the road was our house, which had been a flower mill at one time. We also had lots of room for a barn, barnyard, large winter garden, and big orchard. Across the road was the pasture land where Dad grazed the cattle. The Nith River, which branched off the Grand River, flowed through this portion of land. It was all bush and trees.

We lived a very primitive lifestyle on this farm. There was no plumbing, except for the hand pump in the kitchen, where Dad installed a sink with taps immediately after moving in. We used a five-gallon pail for our toilet, which seldom got emptied. We had electricity. There was no basement until much later. There was a wood burning stove in the corner of the kitchen, which was replaced with an oil stove late in the fall of our first year there.

Living in a literal rat's nest meant major repairs. In order to winterize the house, Dad had to cover up the large holes in the outside walls. It was at this time that I heard Jesus' name for the first time in our home. Dad had a hammer; he was working hard to cover up the major holes one day when he hit his finger. At this point, he used the Lord's name in vain. I giggled and repeated the word. Both my mom and dad glared at me, and with anger in their voices said, "You will go to hell for that."

Dad had made his dream come true. He finally had his farm— but he still had an empty barn. He worked for the Ford plant in Oakville, Ontario. Even though his paycheques were good, he was just squeaking by week to week. He would go to the livestock auction barn with the little cash he had in his pocket, hoping his luck would pay off. He tried a few times without success and came home with empty arms. Sometimes the whole family would go with him to the sales barn.

One day, it happened that only Dad went. A farmer had a three-day-old purebred Jersey calf. He knew the calf was going to die, so he thought he would try to get some cash for her. She was not sucking from her mother and she could not stand on her legs. To add to this, the veterinarian told the farmer that the calf had a bad heart. She was not going to live more than three days.

The helpless calf was carried out and put in the straw were she lay. She did not even have the strength to lift her head and bawl. In all honesty, the auctioneer told the total truth. He started to auction off the calf, but not one farmer would bid. That was when my dad offered the only cash he had in his pocket. He went and got his calf.

Back in the 50s and 60s, farmers would sit at their vehicles selling and giving away puppies and small livestock. On his way to our car, Dad saw in the trunk of a car a pup lying in a bed of straw. She was a total mess. The pup's coat of hair had never been combed and was full of tangles. She had been lying in her own feces. She was all skin and bones. Dad finished taking his calf to the car, then headed back to check out the pup.

When inquiring about the pup, he found out she was six months old. From the way she cowered back when this man stepped near her, my dad got the feeling she had been abused by him. Dad told the man that he had no cash, but he let Dad have the pup, just to take it away. When Dad came in the house, us girls were in the kitchen with Mom. He asked for a blanket and laid the lifeless little calf on the blanket near the wood burning stove. He told Mom that he needed the powered milk made and warmed up to the temperature of a baby's bottle.

While the milk warmed, he went back out to the car and brought in the pup. The pup was fed and made comfortable. However, keeping the calf alive was of the utmost importance, so he returned his focus on to the calf. I am sure us girls would have tried to warm up to the pup, but this would have been of no success, since she was so timid. She was cowering in the corner at the other end of the kitchen, shivering with fear. This is where she was still lying when we went to bed.

Dad put his finger into the warm milk and then proceeded to try to get the calf to suck. When this did not work, he started to pour small dribbles of warm milk into her mouth. After a short time of doing this, the calf started to respond to the milk. Dad also had Mom bring him one of Sherry's baby bottles. Dad made a larger hole in the nipple so that the calf could feed from it. Now that she was ready to accept the milk, he again dipped his finger in. This time, the calf tried. Then Dad gave the baby bottle to her, and she accepted it just fine.

My mother was not the kind of person who would be a caregiver. She would have preferred to be waited on. So even if Dad had asked, she would never had stayed up or taken shifts with him to care for the calf. Our mother and us girls went to bed while Dad stayed up with the calf and pup.

We were all early risers on the farm, so we would all be up to get Dad off to work. When I came down to the kitchen the next morning, it was nice and warm. There was no need to start the wood stove; it had been lit all night. The calf was resting peacefully on the blanket next to the stove. She was covered with a blanket. The pup was bathed and combed out; she was no longer huddled in a corner shivering with fear. Instead, she lied next to Dad on the floor.

Dad looked exhausted, but unconcerned. He was stroking the pup as he looked up at Mom and said, "Now that she is cleaned up, I can see she is a fine looking Collie." Her coat was black, white, and sandy brown—so he named her Sandy. Dad gave Mom instructions on how to care for the calf and then headed off to work. The next two weeks would be a repetition of this first night. He stayed up with the calf every night, keeping the fire lit.

While Dad was at work; Sandy waited for him in the kitchen, at the back door. She also started to warm up to us girls—even Mom. At the end of the two weeks, the calf was standing on her own. Now my dad had full confidence that she would be just fine. It was then that Dad said, "This calf has been nothing but trouble for me. I will name her Trouble." For the last two weeks, he had not slept at all. It would be many years later that Dad would tell us he was falling asleep at the steering wheel and driving to and from work. That winter, Trouble would live in the kitchen, because it was too cold for her in the barn.

He slowly built up the farm by purchasing ducklings and chicks. Again, the small livestock was kept warm in the house.

The oven would be turned on to a low temperature with the door left open. Dad used the oven as an incubator for the small livestock. Later, there would be tiny piglets as well. These would be in the oven, too, to be kept incubated. Therefore, in my early childhood years, our house was often used as a barn.

My parents were not clean people. The house always smelled like a barn. The floors—especially the kitchen floor—only got washed when we had guests. When they would comment on how dirty the floor looked, it would embarrass Dad. Then he would wash the floor. It would not be washed again until another guest commented on it.

The five-gallon pail we used for a toilet was kept in a small walk-in closet under the stairway. Dad would empty it when it was full!

On one occasion, however, Dad again let the pail get to this unpleasant point where we were sitting in our own human waste. It was winter and there had been an ice storm. At my protest, after sitting in this undesirable stench, Dad finally took the pail out back to dump it. Stepping out the door, he stepped onto a clear sheet of ice. One of his legs slid out from under him; he lost his balance and went down. The pail came down on top of him. Mom rushed out to see the pail overturned on Dad's head. As she pulled the pail off, she saw that the contents had dumped all over him, completely covering him with our poo. Dad was one sorry sight to see. After that, he installed indoor plumbing. Then we had a real bathroom, with flowing water, a sink, a bathtub, and a toilet.

I detested living in that smelly, dirty house. For some reason, it did not bother my sisters or my parents, but I liked things picked up and tidied. I could not even stand my hands being sticky or mucky. I would try to tidy papers on the kitchen table and Dad would tell me to leave it alone, that I was disorganizing everything on him. It was a mess; there was nothing organized about it.

He caught me one time trying to clean the heavy, caked-in muck that was layered in between the leaves of the kitchen table. He raised his voice at me and said, "Don't touch that. It is there to prevent the milk and juice from leaking onto the floor when it is spilt." When he would say things like that, it did not register with me. I was abhorrent at the filth.

All efforts to clean and organize the main living quarters failed. But my bedroom was my own room to care for. Starting at the age of four years old, I kept my room immaculate. I never failed to make my bed. I did not like one thing unorganized or untidy. It did not take more than one week before my dad came into my room to see what I had been doing. He was so impressed with me that he started giving me an allowance of twenty-five cents a week for keeping my room tidy.

It did not take me long to start learning the merit of saving. I soon had a penny jar in my bedroom. I took joy in saving my coins, and any small bills. My dad wanted me to just save my coins, but I had different plans. Then my Aunt Helen came to visit us. She had a pretty white vinyl purse. I had never seen anything so pretty. I knew now what I was saving my money for. I asked her where she got the purse and told her how lovely it was. She smiled sweetly and told me I would find one just like hers in the mall in Brantford. I told her I was saving my money for something nice, and now I knew what I wanted. Aunt Helen asked me how much I had saved. She sat down on my bed with me and helped count out my coins. She told me that I did not quite have enough, and then she gave me a whole dollar. I'd never had a dollar before. That was really great!

Then she told me how much I would need to purchase my purse. I was seventy-five cents short. In three weeks' time, Dad would give me three quarters for keeping my room nice. I was so looking forward to this. I did not say a word to Dad until I had enough coins for my purse. When I did tell him, he didn't take it well. I was again reminded that I was the misfit. He had wanted a boy really bad. I was supposed to have been born on St. Patrick's Day, not March 22. I was supposed to be a boy, not a girl. My name was supposed to be Patrick, not Patricia. I was supposed to want toy guns or a toy car, not a purse. He again reminded me that I was that prostitute's misfit. He went to Aunt Helen and told her off for putting the idea in my head. She told my dad to grow up and just let me be a little girl. Dad swallowed his pride and took me to get my purse.

As a small child, this was one of the most exciting days of my life. I hadn't known a store could be so big and bright. The lights lit up everything. We had been in the five and dime stores, but they were dark and dingy. And they were small, like our corner stores today. There was no end to this one—there were rows upon rows of pretty, new items. I thought as we walked through this huge store that it would take a day or more to see everything. I was amazed and excited. No words or expressions could explain my feelings as I walked through that amazing building.

That's when I saw it—just like Aunt Helen's purse only smaller, just right for me. It was a white vinyl purse with a gold chain strap. Dad was not going to give up yet. He gave it one more try, saying, "Pattie, would you not prefer a toy car?" I looked up at him and said, "No, Daddy, this is what I want." When we came up to the teller, I pulled out my bag of change. Outside of the dollar Aunt Helen had gave me, Dad had been giving me quarters. When Dad came and told me he would take me to get my purse, he also told me, "You should take pennies to the store. The teller would be much happier if you brought pennies." And he exchanged me pennies for my shiny silver quarters.

I turned my bag of coins upside-down on the counter. All the pennies fell out. The nice young lady at the till smiled at me. I knew when she smiled that she was very happy with my pennies. I told her that my daddy had said she would be happy with pennies. She told Dad that he could help her count them. The teller and my dad counted all the pennies. There were one hundred and fifty pennies. She took the dollar that Aunt Helen had given me, too. Then I walked out holding my purse, the very first thing I ever bought with my very own money.

When we got back to the house, Dad told Mom that he hadn't thought the teller would take all those pennies. He also told Mom that he had never been so proud of me as he was that day. I looked up and said, "See, Daddy? It tuned out good."

Every time we went out, I took my purse. I had a pretty handbag. I was a big girl, just like Mom. It got old, worn, and tattered, and has long since been lost with my childhood dreams, but still today I can remember every detail of my very first purse.

# CHAPTER 2

# GROWING UP ON A SMALL FARM

*T*he back entrance of our home was on the left side of the house. We entered through the kitchen. On the right-hand side was the wood burning stove, and next to it was the kitchen table. The location of the table would be changed in the middle of the first winter we were there. At that time, the kitchen table was moved so that it was located right across from the back door. Dad built a bay window above the table. Where the table had been, he hooked up an oil furnace. He also got rid of the wood burning stove. The entrance to the hallway was located on the left-hand side of the oil furnace. Next to that was the stairway, which led up to the upper level. On the left side as you entered through the back door were the kitchen cabinets and sink. Above the sink was a window that over looked the barnyard. The refrigerator and stove were located on this wall as well. When you entered from the kitchen in to the hall way, there were two closet doors. The first was like a crawlspace; we kept our toys in this closet. The next closet was big enough to stand up in. This was where our five-gallon pail was kept, which was used as a toilet. A black telephone hung on the wall next to the walk-in closet. Across from the closet was a door that led into a small bedroom. This was where Cathy and Sherry slept. At the end of this hall was our living room. Right across from here was the front door, which led out to the veranda. The veranda spread the full length of the house. On both sides of the front door were identical windows.

Although she never told me this, I believe Mom was afraid of the rats that ran across the steps late at night. When Dad would work the afternoon shift, she would keep me up with her late at night. She would not walk up the steps by herself. I had to go with her when she did the steps. Keeping me up late meant I watched the late night shows, which I was terrified of. Mom only watched horror movies, and she watched the worst ones. After staying up late to watch these late night movies, we would make our way up the steps, which was a horror story of its own.

I don't know why, but Mom would always close the door at the bottom of the staircase. If it was for fear of the rats, it made no sense, because the two younger ones were downstairs sleeping. The door was old and worn. What was once fresh white paint was now yellowed and dirty. The walls on the side of the stairway were white, and cracked. The plaster was separating from the wall, exposing the horse hair and slats that ran horizontal on the wall. The steps were worn-out boards. As we would head up the steps, they would creak loudly. I was afraid it would wake the rats and they would come out. But I never saw them. I thought maybe they knew we were there, and hid from us. Nevertheless, Mom and Dad talked all the time about them, so I did not like walking up the steps at night.

At the top of the stairs was a hallway. Right across from the stairs was a door that was never opened. I did not know what was in that room. To the left was the outside wall. To the right was the hallway, and Mom and Dad's bedroom door was on the right-hand side. My bedroom door was at the very end of the hall. The floors upstairs were the same as the stairs, all old wooden boards. There were holes in the floor; you could see the floor joists. They were deliberately made to let the heat rise from the downstairs. If you looked down in to the open space, there was another hole through the ceiling. This helped to bring the heat from the first floor. There were four of these holes upstairs.

From the moment I would step onto the bottom stair to the moment my foot left the top one, I was terrified. Mom and Dad would talk when our little ears were in listening distance about how rats would chew baby's flesh off its face for the taste of the milk, and that if there were enough of them the rats would gather in a large group and kill, eating the flesh off a small child. The fear did not end there. As I lay in my bed, I thought about them. I thought about my little sisters downstairs alone.

One night, Mom had only a kerosene lamp lit. The television was off. The electricity must have gone out that night. She brought out a cardboard box and then started to cut one whole side of the box off. She used this side to make walls to stand up on the inside of the box. On the outside, she cut out holes for windows and doors. When she was finished this part, it looked like a dollhouse. The back of the house was fully open, so you could look inside. This house she made for me even had a sloped roof on top. She made glue from flour and water. We always had Sears and Eaton's catalogues in the house, because this was how Mom mainly shopped. She brought out the catalogues and started to show me how to cut out the pictures to make it look like a real dollhouse. She had me cut out a picture of a kitchen table and chairs. Then she glued it into the dollhouse. We did the same with pictures of bedroom sets, sofas, and chairs. After the house was decorated, she had me cut out paper dolls to play with.

Suddenly she took a strand of my thick black hair in her hand. She smiled at me and said, "As a baby you had the most beautiful golden blond ringlets. I have never forgiven myself for the day I cut a lock of your hair to put it away. You were six months old when I did it, and after that your hair went straight and black." I stopped cutting and looked up into to Mom's tender eyes. She was still running her fingers through my hair as she continued, "You were the most beautiful baby. It hurt so much, I never thought the pain would ever go away. But then I held you, and all the pain was gone." That was when the lights came on, she got up, and said no more about it.

For many years, I thought she meant the pain from being in labour with me. But I did not fully understand until later that the pain she spoke of was the rape she went through. She carried a baby, conceived out of rape, and yet she could still love me. Today, I wish I could hold her in my arms.

Sunday night was bath night. Dad would fill up the laundry tub with water. He would bathe us girls while we all watched *Bonanza* on the television. It was around this time that Dad started keeping me up later than the other girls. He told me I was his special little girl. Mom would go to bed and leave me downstairs alone with Dad. He taught me how to make eggnogs. I really thought I was my daddy's special little girl.

One day while I was sitting on the floor playing with my dolls and Mom was busy in the kitchen, I had my cut-out dolls all naked. The naked Daddy doll laid on his back. The naked little girl doll laid on her tummy on top of the Daddy doll, so that they were facing each other. Mom watched as I played, and she saw how I had my dolls set up. She then asked me where I learned this. I told her, "Daddy told me it is okay for daddies and mommies to do this. And it is okay for daddies and little girls to do this, and for mommies and little boys to do this. But daddies and little boys don't do this, and mommies and little girls don't do this."

She suddenly got so angry that she scared me. She went storming out of the room. When she came back in, she was shouting at me. I did not understand what I had done that was so bad. It was like she was angry at me! She said, "Don't you ever sit on your daddy's lap again. You don't cuddle up to him. And neither will you stay up late with him."

Mom got real cold towards me. The only time before that I ever remembered that she did touch me in a tender way was the night the electricity went out, but now it was even worse. She would not have me stay up with her at night. She started showing a lot of favouritism to Sherry. It was like I was suddenly a stench to her.

Dad also touched us girls in our private place. He said that it was a game. He told us he was playing with us. When he did this, he would have us girls watch as he would touch one of us. We started acting out on each other the same things he was doing to us. Both Dad and Mom came into the room once and caught us doing this. Mom asked Dad, "Where would the girls learn that?" We spoke up and said, "Daddy plays this game with us."

Before another word could be spoken, Dad said, "Little girls should not be doing that. It is disgraceful."

Dad tried to get close to me, but I was afraid of Mom. I told him what I did with my dolls and cut-outs, and what she had said. He looked really hurt, and after this he would not warm up to me. Dad started to call Cathy his special little girl and started keeping her up late with him. When he would show favouritism to Cathy, it was like he was trying to use this to hurt me.

Aunt Norma lived a long way away from us. As I said, she was the only person who was showing me any affection.

Cathy was light on her feet, and naturally good at dancing. Dad would point that out. If I tried to dance like Cathy, he would say I was clumsy and that I should not even bother, that I looked foolish. To rub it in even further, he paid for Cathy to have dancing lessons. From the day I told Dad what Mom had demanded of me to the day he passed away, no matter how hard I tried to make him proud of me, I never did gain back his approval.

I had a memory of the assault between my dad and me. But it was strange how I would remember it. In my memory, I was looking across the room. I could see Dad lying naked on the sofa, and I was naked, lying on top of him. It was like I was watching this from six feet away. I thought maybe it was just my imagination.

Many years later, after us girls were grown up and had families of our own, a friend came to me in secret. She was troubled about my sister's child. She was so upset that she was ready to call the Children's Aid, but she wanted to bring the problem to me first. She told me that she had walked into my sister's home and seen her lying naked on her back on the sofa. Her child was lying naked facedown on top of her. I asked this person what my sister told her she was doing. She told me that my sister had said she didn't know why she did it; she just thought it was a way to be affectionate with her child. I told this friend not to do anything about it. I said, "I will go to her and talk to her about this." That was the last this friend ever said about this. I knew then that this strange vision was very real. I also knew Dad had not just done it to me. I went to my sister and explained to her that this was not an appropriate way to love her child. I told her that Dad had done the same thing to me. I gave her a hug, and told her that she should not blame herself—because she did not understand how serious this offence was. My sister had no memory of Dad assaulting her.

We grew up in a home where alcohol was badly abused. Every Sunday morning was the same. We would get up in the morning to a bunch of empty beer bottles with cigarette butts dropped in them. These bottles were scattered everywhere. The house stank of stale beer. Even though I was just a small child, I felt that the things Dad would say were not proper. It bothered me to hear his comments about what they had done the night before. While they picked up the bottles, Dad asked Mom, "Did you know that when Hilda came out in that blanket, and wrapped it around me to dance, she had no clothes under it?" This gave me an idea just what their parties were like. The alcohol abuse would only get worse as time went by.

Dad was a Casanova with women. His promiscuous lifestyle was well-paraded in our home. Today I wonder how Mom lived with his wicked ways. I believe it was for the love of her children. But also there was no support for women back in the

50s and 60s like there is today. She would never have survived on her own with three small children. She would have lacked the understanding of what was out there for support.

It would often happen that there would be a shapely, attractive woman in the house. The woman and Dad would flirt back and forth with each other. It never made any difference that Mom was in the room. He was a very attractive man, with his thick dark hair and handsome features. He had a slight crook to his mouth when he smiled that made the women weak in the knees. My Dad was a womanizer. He would manipulate a woman to get anything he wanted.

I would watch him in the store, for instance. As he stood at the counter, he would flirt with the cashier. He would seduce her by leaning over the counter and smiling as he looked steadily into her eyes. His talk was smooth and seductive. Like a serpent after its prey, he would draw her in. It was as though she was hypnotized by his gaze. She was helpless as she stared back into his eyes. Now that he had his victim, it was a case of keeping her gaze on his eyes, and not on his hand. Looking her right in the eyes, he slowly and smoothly moved his hand up to the candies. He slipped his fingers around a candy package and drew his hand back, slipping it into his pocket. Once he had what he wanted, he would straighten his posture and break eye contact.

With no apparent purpose, I would find myself suddenly feeling like I was ready to break out in tears. I was not comfortable crying when people were present in the room with me. On the farm in Canning, there was a rotted tree stump behind the barn. This was located next to the winter garden. When I felt this way, I would go to the tree stump. This is where I would sit and cry. I could get away with it when it was just Mom and Dad at home. They never noticed I was missing. I would stay there until the feeling left. Then I would return to the house, and no one would be the wiser.

One day this heavy feeling came over me while we had a babysitter in to watch us girls. Of course, I did not want the sitter to see me cry. So like all the other times I went to my secret place. But unlike Mom and Dad, she noticed I was missing. When I came back from my tree stump, there was a police car in our driveway. The police officers were just getting out of the car. Dad was shouting at the babysitter, and she was crying. Cathy and Sherry were crying as well. Mom was ringing her hands and pacing the ground. As I came around the corner of the barn, one of the officers pointed at me and asked, "Is this the missing child?" I was in a lot of trouble for that. And the babysitter was in even more trouble than I was.

The next time I went to my tree stump, Dad followed me. He sat down with me and talked softly to me so that I would stop crying. He told me that I did not have to run and hide when I needed to cry. Now I knew he would look for me in that place, so I decided I had to find a new hiding place. After this, when I needed to cry, I started hiding in the thick bushes and trees across the road. It was not so easy to find me in there.

Once in a while a person would come into my life who would just naturally be kind to me, and would intend me no harm. One particular young man was one of these special people in my life. I remember him well. He would have been in his early twenties. Dad had bought me a pony. It was much too frisky for me, and I was afraid of it. Because he was so busy with the farm and the Ford plant, he quite simply did not have time for me and the pony. Therefore, he hired this young man to saddle my pony and give me pony rides. It was agreed that he would not take me off the farm. This man was very kind and gentle-hearted. Even though I told him of my fear of the pony, he did not belittle me or act unkind, like Dad would have done.

His mother was very sick. He was seeking for something, or someone, to make her smile and feel a little bit more cheerful. I guess when he saw me, he thought a little girl was just what his mother needed. So every day he would saddle up my pony and take me home with him. The first time I went into their home, his mother corrected him. She told him, "You will get in trouble for this. You had better take her home." He told his mother he had chores to do and he wanted me to stay in the house with her. She smiled at me and told him to do his chores. She could not get up and do very much, so she told me where the cookies were and how to get myself some milk. I liked her. She was such a nice lady. When her son came in, she thanked him for bringing me to sit with her. She was smiling.

On my way back home, he told me that he had not seen his mother smile for a long time. He thanked me for giving his mother some happiness. He would take me back to his home every morning. I would sit and talk to his mom. Apparently his mom had told him that I gave her joy and that she really liked me being there with her. For me, it was nice to have someone who was good to me. So really, I needed her, too. I looked forward to my mornings with her.

Then one day, Mom noticed I was missing. He took me back home after visiting his mother. Like always, he did no harm to me. Dad got angry and accused him of doing something bad to me. Dad was accusing him of doing to me the very bad things he himself was doing to me. I told Dad the man had never done anything bad. I also told Dad about his mother, and my visits with her. But he would not listen to me. He punished me by giving my pony to Cathy. And he fired the young man. I never saw his mother or him again.

My sisters and I were invited to go to Sunday School. The services were held in a little house in Canning. We went the first Sunday in play clothes. Mom and Dad were not in the habit of going to church, so this was all we had to wear. The pastor would teach us on a flannel board. This was the first time I heard about Jesus without it being a curse word. I was amazed when he said that word. I told him that Mom and Dad had told me I would go to hell if I said that word.

When we came home that afternoon, Mom and Dad were waiting in the kitchen for us. Dinner was ready and on the table. We did not have to be pushed to go to Sunday School. We enjoyed the service so much that us girls continued to go every Sunday. After our third Sunday, Dad had a lady come into our home with a big bundle of pretty dresses. He had us try on the dresses. Cathy and Sherry each got a pretty dress, and then he had to choose between a blue silk dress or a red velvet dress for me. Dad decided on the red velvet dress. These would be the dresses we would wear for Sunday School. We wore the same dresses every Sunday. When we came home, we would immediately change back into our play clothes. Our dresses were only to be worn for Sunday School.

It was Christmas Eve. My sisters and I had now been attending this little church for six months. The pastor had invited Mom and Dad out to the Christmas Eve service. It was highly unusual that they would attend church for any occasion. The only time we had ever attended church as a family was for the baptism of one of us girls, or when we would visit Grampa Campbell at Easter or Christmas.

On this night, Mom and Dad came out to our Sunday School service with us. It was customary of our pastor to do the story on the felt board. This occasion would prove to be no different. He told us about the first Christmas, and the Baby Jesus born in a barn and laid in a manger. He said that this was what Christmas was all about. I listened in silence. I was intrigued over this story. No one had ever told me about the Baby Jesus.

When we got home that night, I sat on the floor and looked up at the colourful lights on the tree. I could not stop thinking about Jesus in the manger. In our home, Santa Claus had been the main focus. From September through Boxing Day, Santa was all Mom talked about. In September, she would start off by telling us about little elves no bigger than the nail on my pinkie finger. She kept pointing to the corner of the window pane, asking, "Don't you see the little elves? They're in the window. They can see you. If you do anything bad, they will tell Santa, and you will get nothing for Christmas."

This Christmas Eve was different from all the others. There was something about the story of Jesus that had my attention.

It was now Christmas morning. Ordinarily, I would have been all excited about Santa and the many gifts that were in the room. My Mom and Dad were like kids at Christmas, and there was never enough room under the tree for all the gifts. Packages wrapped in red and green would be spread across the floor of our living room. A quarter of the room was devoted to Christmas gifts.

But this morning was different from any other Christmas we'd ever had. Like before, the room was just as full of gifts. But the difference was inside of me. All I could think about was the Baby Jesus, in the manger. One of the gifts we opened was a record player. It had all three of our names on it. This gift was intended for us all to share. Each one of us girls also got a small addition to this gift. We received three seven-inch vinyl records. The records were different colours. Some of them were red, some were black, and some were yellow. I especially remembered the two yellow records. One played "Away in the Manger" and the other played "Angels We Have Heard on High." I was a bad girl that morning. As I said, we were expected to share this gift. I kept playing these two records over and over again. The story of Baby Jesus would linger in my head.

For the next few years, I would go to church faithfully every Sunday. Although this pastor of ours believed in having a personal relationship with Jesus, I don't recall at this early stage in my life asking Jesus into my heart. But I do know that I loved this Jesus very much and could not get enough of this teaching.

I noticed that the pastor always prayed. One night, as I was heading off to bed, I told Dad that I wanted to pray at bedtime. He sat down next to me, on my bed, and prayed this prayer. I repeated it after him.

> Now I lay me down to sleep.
> I pray my Lord my soul to keep.
> If I should die before I wake,
> I pray the Lord my soul to take.
> Amen.

After we repeated it enough nights, I had it memorized, so I could say this prayer on my own. I was not satisfied with this. When we sat down to dinner, again I said that I wanted to pray before we eat. Mom and Dad agreed on a little prayer. I suppose both of them would have said this one when they were tiny. The prayer went like this.

> God is good.
> God is great.
> Now we thank him for our food.
> Amen.

We had been attending church for one year when Mom and Dad took us to the Sunday School picnic. When we got there, I noticed the food was ready. I also noticed that everyone was talking and did not seem to notice the food. I thought it was time to pray, so I spoke up loud enough to be heard, "We have to pray now." That was when every eye went to me. Mom and Dad looked embarrassed, but all the others thought I was cute. The pastor picked me up and stood me on the picnic table. He said, "Pattie will lead in prayer today." I said the dinner prayer that Mom and Dad had taught us.

At home, there was an iron gate that Dad had told me over and over again not to touch. He could not get it into my head to leave it alone. The day came when I enticed my younger sisters, to join me in playing with the gate. This time the gate started to come down on my little sisters. I knew the two younger ones were small enough that if the gate came down on them, they would be crushed, so I took the weight of the gate on myself. I held it so that it would not come down on my little sisters, and then I told Cathy and Sherry to get out from under it. I was holding the weight of the gate on my back.

This gate was too heavy for me to hold. It was only a matter of time before it would crush me. I told them to run to Dad and get help. That day, I got the one spanking I would never forget. I thought then that it was unfair, since I had rescued my sisters, but later after I thought it over. I understood that I had been told enough times not to touch it, and I did not listen. Today when I think about it, I know that Jesus protected us that day. If for any reason Dad had not shown up on time, or I had not been able to stop that gate from coming down on my sisters, it is possible I would not have been able to hold the weight of the iron gate. In that case, there would have been angels holding the gate. Nevertheless, all three of us girls could have been seriously hurt. Or worse, we could have been killed.

Until the age of six, I never thought of myself being any different from other children. It would take one year in the school system for me to understand how different I truly was. I remember that I was very afraid of the unknown. My first day of school would prove to be one of the most frightful days of my entire childhood. Mom took me by my hand and walked me to school. Dad must have been home with the younger girls, because they did not come with us.

As we entered the school, the teacher looked directly at me. With anger in her face, and strength in her voice, she thundered, "We don't have dogs in this school. Get it out."

I was so terrified, that I could not even move. Nor could I take my eyes off of this cold, merciless woman. Again she shouted, this time pointing her finger at me, "Get that dog out." Everyone in the class was laughing—I thought maybe they were laughing at me. Mom turned and looked at me. That was when Mom saw Sandy standing directly behind me. With her family she was a sweet, gentle dog, but she would have never let anyone harm us girls. No person in their right mind would have ever touch one of us girls when Sandy was in the room. The teacher forced Mom to put our dog outside.

When Mom left the school, she took Sandy with her. I pleaded with her not to leave me. The teacher snapped at me, "Stop your whining and sit down." I was terrified of this woman. I would have felt better if Sandy had stayed, even though for the teacher's sake it was best that our family pet go home.

It was in a one-room schoolhouse that I attended my first two years of school. There was one large main room, which was our classroom. We entered the schoolhouse from the back of the class. There was no kindergarten. Grade One was the first grade. At the head of the room was a large wooden desk, which belonged to our teacher, Mrs. Defoe. On the left side of her desk, hanging on a pole, was the Canadian flag. It was propped up against the wall, as to dangle loosely. At the top left corner of the flag was the Union Jack. On the right side of the flag was a crest.

On the far wall from my desk was a map of the world. I was fascinated by this, since I had never seen one before. Behind the teacher's desk was a chalkboard that extended the full length of the wall. Next to my desk was a window that looked out over the schoolyard and the road. Every one of the desks had a hole on the right-hand side that at one time had held an inkwell.

I found my natural born talent with our first assignment that morning. The first graders were told to draw a picture of a train car. I am sure the teacher explained herself well. The problem would have been with myself. I had no idea what a train car was. So when she told us to draw a picture of a car, I drew an automobile. This vehicle had wheels, a steering wheel, headlights, back-up lights, and door handles. She looked at my picture, and she was stunned. She just could not get over how perfect this picture had turned out. The honest fact was that I had never drawn before. Outside of scribbling on the wall with black crayon, this was my first time sketching a picture. She was so taken by my picture that when Mom came back for me that afternoon, she remarked on it. But she did not tell my mother everything.

When I saw that the children in each grade worked so hard at their tasks, I thought that the idea was to out-achieve one another. Therefore, I wanted to prove myself the better achiever in the class. Right away, I believed this was the purpose of this room. My desire was to rise above all the other students. Our first assignment would prove my abilities. Mrs. Defoe assigned us first graders our lesson, then she moved over to the Grade Eight class. I tried to focus on my work, but there was continual noise in the room. The teacher was speaking to the eighth graders, pencils were dropping on the floor, children were flipping the pages in their notebooks... every so often, someone would leave their desk to sharpen a pencil. Then there was the grinding of the pencil sharpener or the sound of chalk scraping against the board.

I tried to concentrate on my work, but this would be of no success. That was when I noticed the teacher had a long pointer in her hand. She was showing the Grade Eight students the different continents on the map. This was something I had a curiosity about, so I took my focus off my work and put it onto what she was teaching the older children. When she saw that I was watching what was going on at the other end of the class, she grabbed the strap and came for me. She took my hands and spread them out to give me a strapping. That's when I started to cry. Suddenly Mrs. Defoe stopped and put the strap away. It was after this that I noticed most of the Grade Eight students looking very concerned for me.

That afternoon, as Mom was heading back to the house with me and my sisters, one of the girls from the Grade Eight class came running up to us. She told my mother, "I can see that you have your hands full with three small girls. Would you like me to walk Pattie back and forth to school? I could pick her up at your home and then return her in the afternoon." Mom was more than happy to take her help. Dad was anxious about why a girl that age would want to walk me to and from school rather than hang out with the other girls and boys her own age. However, Mom did have her hands full already, so she argued the point with Dad. She won this battle.

I felt safe with this older girl. She was there every morning and afternoon to walk me back and forth to school. I was afraid of Mrs. Defoe, but knowing this older girl was with me at school me to not be so afraid.

For the next two weeks, she would walk me back and forth. Then one afternoon, after she had brought me home, she sat on the swing that was in the orchard. She was talking to all three of us girls. We were enjoying her company very much when suddenly the swing broke, and she landed on the ground. She must have been afraid that she would be in trouble, because she took off right away. Dad asked me who broke the swing. He had hung the swing in the tree for us. He was very angry. I told him the truth. He did not liked the girl to begin with, so this gave him an excuse to get rid of her. I pleaded with him. I told him how afraid I was of Mrs. Defoe. Mom tried to talk to him as well, but he would not listen to our pleas. He would not let the girl walk me to school anymore. I regretted that I had told him the truth.

Within the first week of school, I started to notice that I could not learn simple activities. Any sound as small as a pen dropping to the floor would break my concentration. I was not able to memorize things. Students started saying I was retarded.

The teacher would ask, "What is wrong with you?" I could not learn to read past the first grader "Dick and Jane" books. I had trouble learning to read. I could read my own spelling, and I certainly could not read a book. When it came to tests, Mom or Dad would have to sit with me and try to help me memorize my notes. I would often fall asleep crying, because I could not do it and I did not want to look like an idiot.

I was the only Grade One student who failed that year. As a matter of fact, from six to sixteen years of age, I never passed one grade. After I got too big, the teachers would just put me on to the next grade to avoid embarrassing me any more than was necessary. I did Grade One three times. It was very uncomfortable to be in the same class as my little sister, who was three years younger than me. And it seemed like everyone liked to rub this in.

My mother and father were no exception to the rule. After so many years, I just gave up and started waiting for the day that I would no longer have to go to school.

Two years after I started school, the school board closed the one-room schoolhouse and everyone who lived in the village of Canning then had to be bussed to Princeton, where the school had single rooms for every class. The dunce desk was always in the back row on the right side of the room. This was where I was always seated. It was known by all the teachers that I could not learn. But it was also known that I was a natural-born artist and that I could sketch anything that was put before me. Therefore, every one of my teachers over the years would use me to sketch their art exhibits for the fall fair. This one particular teacher got greedy and held me back one year so that she could have her exhibit in the fair two years in a row. My parents went to the school board and had her forced to move me to the next grade.

One particular Sunday morning started off like all the others. We were dressed and off to church. This time when we came in there was a delicious smell in the kitchen of tarts, cookies, pastries, and many other sweet delights. Like always, everyone went and sat in the living room for the morning service. When our pastor came in, he opened the service in a whole different manner. It did not take long before I knew that I was the guest of honour.

I was called up to the front of the room. Everyone's faces were beaming with excitement as they watched me. The pastor picked up a King James Bible with a black leather cover and handed it to me. He said, "Congratulations on a perfect Sunday School attendance. For three years, you have not missed one Sunday service." This was totally unexpected. I'd had no idea this was going to happen until the pastor handed the Bible to me. My sisters were quite upset with this. They could not understand why I got this and they did not get anything. The pastor explained to them that I had not missed any Sundays, but they had missed a few.

When I got home, I hurried to show Mom and Dad the Bible that I had received. My two sisters came in, and they were crying. My parents paid no attention to me, just to Cathy and Sherry. I took my Bible upstairs, to my bedroom. I was not sure whether or not I would ever be able to read it, or any other book, since I was struggling so much in public school, but I knew I would cherish it forever. Today this Bible sits by my bed.

Two drastic things happened to me at the age of seven. One would not be noticed until a few years later, but the other was very noticeable right away. It happened in the winter of my second year of school, while I was walking home. Although the roads were clear, the bridge that I would cross over to go home was covered in ice. I slipped on the ice and went down. I hit the cement hard enough to cause severe damage to my backbone. I don't know how long I was lying there, but to me it seemed like ages before someone came and picked me up. When I did get home, Mom and Dad accused me of making it sound much worse than what it was. I kept trying to go to bed, but they would tell me to get up and move around. There was very little relief from the pain, even when I lay down, which meant I would be up most of the night crying. I tried to tell them how much it Hurt, but no one would listen to me. I was walking with a bad limp and leaning badly to one side. It was six months before the pain started to let up.

This accident left me with two severe curves in my spine. To look at me from the front, it gave the illusion that there was no hip bone on my one side. On my other side, it looked as though I had an extra wide hip. I was left with a severe limp that I would have to live with for the rest of my life. Many years later, it would be found out that a vertebrae in my spine had been cracked.

Sometime during the same year as my fall on the bridge, my upper jaw stopped growing. The appearance of this would become more evident at the time of my youth. The two things together—my curved spine and deformed jaw—would have a large effect on how other children and youth would treat me as I struggled through my teen years.

Growing up in the late 50s meant we were very limited when it came to what there was to watch on television. Some families had an antenna outside, but often enough they would have bunny ears on top of their TV sets. We had a wire that ran along the wall to bring in the local stations. If the computer had yet been invented, this device had not yet made its way into the public. Neither were there video games. Therefore, children had to be creative with their play. The simplest things could satisfy my wants and needs.

This is where the coffee percolator comes into play.

The coffee percolator was a very simple device to use. In the bottom section of the percolator, the user places the correct amount of water for the amount of coffee they want to make. The basket, into which the ground coffee is placed, is held aloft in the pot by a hollow tube, at the bottom of which is a stand. Water in the bottom of the pot is brought to a boil. The heated water is forced up the center, hollow tube. At the top of the tube, the heated water is dispersed downward by a small glass dome in the lid. This water then, by the force of gravity, goes through the perforated lid on the basket containing the coffee grounds, dribbling through the coffee and leaving the basket through little holes. The brewed coffee is then mixed with the water heated in the bottom of the main pot, where the process begins anew.

Now you ask, play with that? How would I play with it? While Mom and Dad sat in the living room watching *The Lawrence Welk Show*, my sisters and I were expected to wash and dry the dishes. I was putting the dirty dishes in the sink when suddenly, quite by accident, I discovered that if the basket from the percolator was pushed into the sink of clean soapy water, by holding it upside-down, it would make a funny noise and make lots of extra suds. It is a well-known fact that all children love to play with water. As soon as I discovered this new game, there was no stopping me. I had no problem washing dishes. I was having a ball. I was laughing and full of giggles.

It got so that I was not washing dishes at all. After three hours of steady fun, Dad came into the kitchen to see what was taking so long. This was fun, and I was enjoying it—a little too much. My punishment was to sit and watch the television with Mom and Dad, while Sherry and Cathy did the dishes. They argued with Dad that it was not fair. I told him that it was only fair that I should help my younger sisters with the dishes, but there was no winning this battle. We even had a lady friend of Dad's come in, who said, "That is not a punishment. She should be doing dishes." He told her, "Believe me, this is a punishment." Dad would not give in. It was a long time before I did dishes again.

Every Christmas, Mom and Dad had brought in the tree and decorated it after we had gone to bed, so we never had the fun of helping. This Christmas was going to be very special for me, because it was the first time I would be allowed to help decorate the tree. All the years I lived at home, we never had a fake tree. I watched as Dad brought in the tree. It filled the house with the scent of pine. The branches were covered in snow. When he stood it up, the snow shook from the branches onto the floor. The tree was thick and heavy. The branches were full. He laid it down so that he could cut the bottom branches off, to make the tree fit into the pail of sugar and water that would hold it.

Dad took his small saw and started to cut off the bottom branches. Mom brought in some red ribbon and tied it around the branches that had been removed. Dad turned the tree over and put it into the pail. Once he had the tree secure, so it would not come down, Dad and Mom took the decorative branches and attached them to the lintels of the windows and doors. They were hung in the same room as the decorated tree. Next they brought in the ornaments. First they put the lights on the tree. The lights shone brightly in colours of red, green, blue, and amber. Then he brought out his favourite ornament—an angel—and hung it at the very top of the tree. All the years I was growing up, this angel always hung at the top of our Christmas tree. After that it was all the ornaments that Grama Campbell had given us. Dad said that these ornaments had hung on the tree when he was a little boy.

My grandmother's ornaments were made of blown glass. They were all very pretty, in their many colours and shapes, but there was one that stood out more than the others. This one would be my favourite for many years to come. It was a tiny red heart, no larger than an acorn. The paint was badly worn. It was obvious that it had been lovingly favoured for many years. It may have quite possibly been my grandmother's favourite ornament, which only made me favour it even more. When I saw it, right away I asked if I could put it on the tree. To my pleasure, Mom and Dad agreed to let me. After this I would put that same ornament on the tree every year, until we had it no more.

After the glass ornaments were on, Dad wrapped strands of silver around the tree. Next were the icicles. They were made of metal. They were firm and twisted, so that they would not bend. The paint was wearing off on them. They looked old, and I did not think they were the most appealing to look at. Some of them were red, some green, and some were silver. They quite simply disappeared when I was a little older. One year they were there, the next they weren't. Today I believe the metal icicles would be very rare antiques, as I have never again come across icicles of this type—and I spend much of my spare time browsing in antique shops.

Last but not least, the candy canes were hung. Us girls were not allowed to touch these sweet temptations until after the tree came down, which would not be until after New Year's Day.

We had a large wooden console that stretched almost across the full length of our living room wall. On both sides of this cabinet were built-in speakers covered with brown fabric. This cabinet had sliding solid wood doors that concealed the built-in thirty-four inch television screen. There was also a nice size space for storage. A section of the top of the console was on hinges. When you raised this section, it would reveal the record player and radio. Back in the late 50s and early 60s, this was luxurious living. The record player and radio gave us top of the line stereo music. The record player played five long-playing records at one time by dropping one record down at a time from a long stem in the center of the turntable. Therefore, we had continuous Christmas music playing all the time as we were decorating the room.

The next morning was Christmas. Like always, there was no shortage of gifts under the tree. All three of us girls received identical gifts from our Aunty Joice. When I opened my gift, I saw that it was a housecoat. The great fact about this was that it was done in patchwork. And it was a coat of many colours. This was the most marvellous gift I had ever before received or would ever receive again. My heart was totally taken by this wonderful gift. But the best was yet to come.

When we were all finished opening our gifts, Dad was suddenly very hurt. It looked like there was no gift for him under the tree. Mom looked for Dad's gift, but it had somehow gone missing from among the gifts. He was so hurt that he went out to the barn, where he stayed for some time. Mom went through all the disregarded wrapping paper and empty boxes. Then finally she found it. It was a very tiny box. She did not go to Dad; I guess she thought he was doing chores. When he came in, he had been drinking. Mom brought him his Christmas gift, and gave it to him. We were all watching as he opened his gift—fourteen-caret gold cufflinks. Dad and Mom hugged as he started to cry. This was the only time I ever saw them hug.

Today electric kitchen stoves are very simple to hook up. It's as easy plugging the plug into the outlet behind the stove. Back in that day, however, it was more complicated than that. New kitchen stoves came with exposed wires instead of a plug. You had to actually wire it up to the wires in the wall behind the stove. The wires coming from the wall were held within a black plastic coating, as were the wires coming from the stove. You had to tear back the plastic coating in order to expose the wires. This was not a job to be done by a person who had been drinking. Today we would call an electrician to do something of this sort. Dad started to hook up Mom's gift. He was feeling quite tipsy, and therefore connected the wires all backwards. Ones he knew he was defeated, he told Mom that there would be no Christmas dinner roasted in this oven today.

Mom called her sister, our "Aunty Joice," and told her about the problem. She came to our home and took our goose to her home, so that she could cook it for us. Later in the day at dinner hour, she came back with our finished goose. And so Aunty Joice saved the day.

While she was gone, and Dad and Mom were relaxed and not so shook up, they took a closer look at the housecoats that all of us girls had received for Christmas. To them it looked like the housecoats had been handmade, but they would have been complicated to sew, so when our Aunt came back with the roasted bird, Mom and Dad asked her if she had made the housecoats.

She told my mother and father that she had taken and sewed all the individual patches together, then cut it into a pattern to make the housecoats. After this, she put each housecoat together. I was so overwhelmed by this that I went right over and gave my Aunt a hug. I said, "Thank you, Aunty Joice, for my coat of many colours."

For me this was someone who had said I was special. So many times I had heard Dad say that I was not pretty or smart enough to be his daughter—and, of course, there was all the talk about the Italian prostitute. How sad it made me that I was too dumb to learn in school. But now, Aunty Joice was saying through her actions that I was special. This coat was like the coat of many colours that Joseph received from his father, Jacob. I had learned this story on the felt board in the little church that we attended.

I can look back and see many times were God was watching over me. This one occasion happened when we were at the beach for a day. Dad had bought me a black inner tube the day before to play with in the water. Mom and Dad took their eyes off me long enough for me to drift away with the current. By the time they knew I was missing, I was so far out in the lake that there was no way it could be safe for a lifeguard to swim to my rescue. The lifeguard had to take a boat out to rescue me. It is good that I did not panic. I could have easily drowned out there.

As I said, it would be a number of years before I saw my Grampa Ainsworth again. Finally Dad agreed to take us to see him. As we traveled to the hospital, Dad would continue to repeat, "This is what happens when you drink too much." It was like he was thriving on it. Mom was very quiet. All the way there, she did not say a word. I was so looking forward to seeing him. He always made me feel so special.

When we got there, I ran right to Grampa. I was so excited to see him. He did not know any of us. I thought for sure he would remember me, but he did not. He said to the nurse that was attending to him, "See, these sweet little children think I am their Grampa. Look how cute they are!" I know that it must have hurt Mom, but I only noticed the pain that was in my heart. I left feeling hurt that Grampa did not know me. I believed for many years that Dad was right about the drinking.

Then, years later, I knew that he must have simply lost his memory with old age. If this hurt me so much, how much more had this hurt my mom? Not to mention Grampa, who went all those years not seeing his little girl. Grampa died a short time after that. I don't think Dad let Mom go to her own Dad's funeral. I know he told me that I could not go.

One day, I was standing in Mom and Dad's bedroom. They were arguing over sex. Dad wanted to have sex, and Mom did not. He had this white tube in his hand that looked like a syringe without a needle. Dad was shaking it in Mom's face. He was shouting, "Every time you have conceived one of the kids, you had to be raped. You did not even want Pattie. You tried to kill her." Like, *hello!* I was in the room!

The gruesome horror stories that Mom and Dad talked about would give me nightmares. I can remember waking up from terrible dreams. Some of my dreams had a large pack of rats in my bed trying to eat me. I would wake up terrified and have trouble going back to sleep.

One morning I woke up to something that really scared me bad. There was tiny poop droppings on my blanket. I was so afraid that this was a rat. I called Dad into my bedroom and showed the little droppings to him. He told me I did not have to be afraid of this. He said it was only a mouse. He told me that a little mouse would never hurt me. As I said, I did not get a lot of affection at home, so if anyone was willing to show me affection, I was more than eager to receive it. Therefore, when he told me about the mouse, I thought it was on my bed because the tiny little creature liked me.

That night when I went to bed, I took some breadcrumbs with me. I sat up in my bed and waited for the little mouse to return. Sure enough, my little friend came back. I took the bread and tore it into little bits for him to eat. He was so cute as he sat on his tiny hindlegs and held his crumbs with his paws. He ate the little crumbs I gave him. I talked to him. I told him that we could be friends.

For the next two weeks, I would bring my little friend breadcrumbs every night. He would sit on my bed and watch me. I was so afraid of the rats that I did not like sleeping in my bedroom alone. My little friend would comfort me, because he never left until after I fell asleep. Really, just having someone there with me until I fell asleep was enough.

My father believed that one did not have animals for the purpose of having a pet. And living on a farm, that was a good rule. He had seven cats in the house, and just as many in the barn. The whole idea of the cats was to kill the mice and rat population, since we were so overrun by them. Therefore, the cats were not fed. Their food would be whatever they caught.

I knew my mouse was in danger, and it would only be a matter of time before a hungry cat would get it. I had seen the cats kill their prey. It was cruel how they would do it. They would play with the little mouse and terrorize it until the mouse would give up the will to live. And it would die.

This little mouse had gained my friendship, however, so I could not let anything bad happen to him. Not now. I knew I had to keep my secret to myself, because Dad did not like the mice. So in the privacy of my bedroom, I tried to make a mouse trap that was a little pen for him to live in. I thought I could feed my little friend and care for his needs, and he could run on my bed when it was only me and him in the room.

That night was no different. I sat and waited for my friend. He came and sat on my bed. I fed him crumbs. I told him about the cats, but he did not have to worry, because I would take good care of him. I had his pen all set up. When he grabbed the breadcrumbs, it would cause the trap door to come down. I fell asleep with my little friend on my bed, watching me.

I woke up to my mom screaming and stomping her feet on the floor. I looked, and my little mouse had been in his pen. He'd eaten his crumbs and the trapdoor had come down. But the pen was empty. I came around the corner. My mouse was squealing and spinning circles around my mom. She was leaping up and down on the floor while she screamed.

"Mommy, be careful!" I said. "You're going to hurt my mouse."

Later Mom told me that she was just stepping out of bed when the mouse raced around the corner from my bedroom and started spinning circles around her. I don't think my mother was impressed with me. Dad told me that I had done a bad thing, and my little friend never did come back.

There was a movie Mom and I watched. It was called "The Blob." This movie was about a pale blue blob that was in a circular form. It would roll across the ground. When it came up to people or animals, it would suck them in. This was like an energy that made it grow bigger, and as it got bigger it would devour more people. This blob was rolling around on the ground, and people were screaming. This movie terrified me, and for quite some time I could not get it out of my head.

I got up one night in the late hours and headed for the toilet. Just as I came into the kitchen, I saw, in the darkness of the room, the blue reflection that came from the pilot light of the oil burning stove. The reflection was about fourteen inches wide as it reflected on the wall. It looked just like the blob in the movie.

I started screaming. I woke up the whole household. When everyone came into the room, I told them about the movie, and that the blob was going to devour us all. Dad had to show me that it was only the pilot light and that it would not kill or harm anyone.

Only towns and cities had private telephone lines. Anyone living out of town had party lines. This meant you had no guarantee of privacy. Anyone sharing your party line could pick up their receiver and listen in to your private conversations. All individual homes had their own separate code. This is how they knew if the phone call was their phone line or some other. For instance, our code was two short rings followed by one long ring. Eventually, our neighbour next door was on the same party line as us. Her code was three long rings.

There were some on our party line who abused the system. If the person heard the telephone ring, and it was their neighbour's ring, then that person would pick up the receiver and listen in to the person's private conversation. Therefore, the telephone line was a device commonly used for gossip.

I will show you an example of this gossip. Dad had a bad grievance with the lady who lived next door. She did not like him and she took every effort to display her feelings towards him. One particular morning, Dad woke up extra early, because he could not sleep. For some time, he had been trying to figure out how he was going to tear out one of our outside walls so he could put in a window. The house was built in such a way that every idea that came into his head just would not work. But he woke up this morning with the idea to take his John Deere tractor and hook it up to the wall, then tear it out. This tractor had one wheel in the front, plus it was large. It could very easily topple over.

Suddenly Dad was running into the house in a panic. He took off up the steps to his bedroom and woke Mom. He told her to get up, and get all the kids out of the house, as it was going to come down. Mom rushed us all out of our beds. We were all standing outside, in our night clothes, looking at what Dad had done to the house. On the left side of the house, he had taken down one third of the outside wall. The whole left corner of the house was missing. The veranda was also down.

Our neighbour, Mrs. Kischak, must have been watching from her window. Within half an hour, the dirt road we lived on had become like grand central station. The traffic was heavy. Everyone was driving past our house and slowing down to take a better look at what Dad had done. Our dirt road was like a four-lane highway all that day. Even our pastor came to the house that morning. He said that he would pray for us, and asked Dad if he needed any assistance.

I don't know what his first plans were, but he said he had not intended for the house to come down in this manner. He said that he would have to now change his plans. He never did replace the veranda. Where the door and two windows were, Dad put in a large picture window. He moved the front entrance to the right side of the house and never did put a window where I believed he had originally intended.

Because of the problem I had with learning, I was very much a loner. It was not easy for me to make friends, and I kept very much to myself. One time, my dad made friends with a nearby farmer. His daughter went to Princeton school. She was the same age as me. Every weekend, we would go as a family to visit this friend of Dad's. This gave me and this girl a chance to get to know each other. Her father was totally gross, and he did some things in a very vulgar way. Like us, he had a five-gallon pail that he used for a toilet. But unlike us, he had no private place to keep it. His toilet sat in the corner of the kitchen, next to the back door. It did not matter that he had guests or not—his wife, himself, and all his sons and daughters were to use the toilet in the presence of every person who came to visit. I guess he thought that if the animals could do it, why not us? So if you were sitting at the kitchen table, they would just pull down their pants and sit on the toilet.

His daughter that was my age was the only sane one in this household. She did not like sitting on the toilet with a full room of people watching. She kept a china pot upstairs were she could use the bathroom in privacy. As shy as I was, the point was this:

I either made friends with his daughter or used this pail—and there was no way that I was going to use that pail. Upstairs were the bed rooms, if you could call them that. He had the bedrooms framed off, but there was no drywall up. Therefore, they only had two-by-fours for walls.

The oldest of the boys was getting girl-crazy, so when my friend would take me upstairs to use her chamber pot, he would follow us so that he could watch us go to the bathroom. She would start shouting at him and he would go downstairs only after his father and mother told him to leave us girls alone.

There was a room off of the kitchen that we would play in. There was a pot belly stove and table in that room. Sometimes we would sit on the floor and play "Barrel Full of Monkeys." Other times, we would play really old records. These records played music from back in the 30s. Other times we would cut up her grandmother's old dresses and make doll clothes. We became good friends, and we would hang out together at school. It was really nice to have a friend. Not only that, but she was my best friend.

One night, when we were making dresses for her dolls, she told me that someday she wanted to have a pretty blue dress that had printed flowers on it. She said that they were poor and that she had never had a pretty dress.

A few days later, my mom called me over after hanging up the phone. She looked concerned. She came into my room and told me, "You had better sit down." She sat next to me. "Your friend has been in an accident. She was with her brothers in the loft of the barn, where they were playing a game. They were jumping across a three-foot wide hole in the floor of the loft. When it was her turn to jump, she lost her balance. She fell two stories on to the cement floor below, head first. Your friend is now in the hospital. She is in a coma."

We waited by the phone for what seemed like a long time. When they did call back, Dad was told that she had died. The doctor said that if she had lived, she would have been a vegetable. She would not have been capable of doing anything. Twelve hours after she fell, she died.

I went to her funeral. She was in a blue coffin, and she wore a pretty blue dress that had printed flowers on it. I heard Mom and Dad talking about the funeral. They said that someone had paid for all of it, because her parents could not afford anything more than a cardboard box.

Can anyone understand the pain of losing a child unless they have lost one of their own? What if you lost every one of your children, in the matter of a few minutes? Aunt Norma and Uncle John had two children. Linda was the oldest. She was in her second year of public school. Johny was their baby, and he had just started school that fall. Their children were the apple of their eyes. My uncle had put in a vegetable garden across the road. My aunt was busy in the kitchen preparing dinner. She needed tomatoes, and so she sent Linda and Johny across the road for the tomatoes. Uncle John saw the drunk driver hit their kids. One of them died instantly at the road. The other died on the way to the hospital.

I can only remember standing at the grave as they let down the coffins of both Johny and Linda. It was a dark and dismal day. You could feel the pain that was felt by every person standing at that cold, cruel grave.

The next time we went to visit them, I noticed right away the sadness in my aunt's eyes. My uncle looked so withdrawn. I thought about how Mom did not seem to want me the way she wanted the other girls and how Dad always said I was not pretty or smart enough to be his daughter. I was sure neither of them wanted me, and it looked to me like Aunt Norma and Uncle John needed a little child very much. My aunt always cuddled me, and therefore I believed she loved to cuddle children. And now she had none of her own to hold close to her. I thought that there would never be a more opportune time than now to offer my aunt the opportunity of a life time.

I pulled up close to her and snuggled my face into her chest. That was when she started to cry. I wiped her cheek with my fingers and said, "Don't cry, Aunt Norma. I will be your little girl. I will come and live with you and Uncle John." My uncle snapped at her, "Now look what you have done." My aunt got very quiet. I had this feeling that I should never have said this.

When we came to visit them again, they had bought a new house and they were full of joy. I guess I must have given them an idea, because they had adopted three children. These children were wards of the foster care system and they were all brothers and sisters. They would have ordinarily have had no hope of being adopted into the same home. Aunt Norma and Uncle John gave all three of these children a home. I could see how happy everyone looked.

I was so full of envy for what these children had. If only I could have had even the crumb that fell from their plate. After they adopted their new family, my aunt never cuddled me again. Mom and Dad said that the three children saved their marriage. Up until they adopted the children, they were blaming each other for the death of their son and daughter.

Every night after we went to bed, I could hear my mom and dad fighting. This frightened me. I thought perhaps they would split up, and then what would happen to us girls?

# CHAPTER 3

# TWO NEW BABIES

*M*y mother's tummy was starting to get quite big and she was wearing smock tops. It was when she started wearing these tops that we were told Mom was going to have another baby. I was not real excited about this. I was more interested in cutting up her maternity tops into doll clothes. I had remembered playing with my friend and her dolls, and I thought I would like to do the same thing. I was very innocent as I asked her if, after she gave birth to the baby, I could have the maternity tops for this purpose. She started to cry, then went to Dad and told him that I had said I wanted her dead.

Why would I wish my mother to die? I was shocked and ashamed for asking for doll clothes. Dad looked at me like I had done something bad. I don't know why, but that day I felt a distance develop between my mother and me. I now understand morning sickness and postpartum depression, but then I felt very badly misunderstood.

It was in her midterm that we found out she was expecting twins.

There is some confusion as to where we stayed when the babies came. While our mother was in the hospital giving birth to the twins, I have no memory of staying at our Aunty Joice's home. However, my sisters say they remember staying there. I remember Dad teaching me how to make a meal for him, so that when he came home from work he would have his dinner ready. I also remember that he taught me to sew a button onto his shirt, so I believe that I stayed at home with Dad.

The first I can remember of the twins was when we were traveling home in the car. Cathy and Sherry were sitting in the back seat. Dad had me sit in the front seat in between him and Mom. Mom held the baby girl, and I was holding the baby boy. They were wrapped in fresh-knitted white blankets and they were sleeping peacefully. Neither of the babies had yet been named. Dad asked if Cathy and I would like to name them. I am very sure if we had given them names like Mitts or Fluffy, he would have put a stop to it right there, but my sister named the girl Tamara Lynne (which, now that I think about it, had a pretty and lacy sound to it), and I named the boy Richard James, which sounded strong and masculine. Both our mother and father was very pleased with our choices in names. Therefore, the names we chose stuck.

They had two cribs, but neither of the babies weight was more than four pounds, eleven ounces. Therefore, to begin with Dad put only one crib up. Tammy lay at the one end and Ricky lay at the other. Mom had been picking up the girl and handling her, but she had not yet picked up the boy. He started to cry. She would not touch him. Dad said, "Pick up the baby!" She said, "No, I will not touch him." This could have started into another fight, but instead Dad told me to go and get my Thumbelina doll. When I brought my doll to him, he put it in the crib next to Ricky and said, "Do you see, Pattie, how much the doll looks like the baby?" Then Dad told me to take my doll and give it to Cathy. He told me, "The baby is now your doll."

To explain this better, I should say that I was a very inquisitive child. Every one of us girls had a Thumbelina doll. I wanted to know what made my doll move and what made the music play, so I had torn Cathy's doll apart. She was still very unhappy with me, so this way she got my doll—and I got the real baby. I had no complaints about giving up my doll for this cooing, cuddly baby. Dad told me that I would be responsible for everything except the baby's bath. He said that he could take care of that. I would learn to feed him and change his diaper. Dad picked him up and put the little boy in my arms.

The twins were born in September 1964. I was ten years old. I noticed right from the start that Mom never held Tammy when it was time for their feeding. Instead she would prop the bottle up with a blanket and let the baby feed itself. Since I was very young and knew nothing about babies, I just did the same with Ricky.

After the birth of the twins, our father and mother decided it was best that they take their parties elsewhere. They started going to Mr. and Mrs. Vandenburge's house to party. Dad was very satisfied with how well I was doing with Ricky, and therefore thought it would not hurt to have me sit with the kids. Mom was concerned at first, but after I had one good night babysitting my sisters and brother, she felt okay with it. Now I had someone to cuddle with, someone I could love, someone who would love me back.

The next two years were the best years of my childhood. Most young girls love babies, and I was no exception to this rule. From the first moment I held him, Ricky stole my heart. Sitting in the car with my little brother in my arms gave me a warm, motherly feeling. Later when Dad told me he would be my baby doll to take care of, I could never have imagined a more perfect gift. I knew then that I would cherish him forever. When Dad offered me the baby in place of the doll, Ricky had me—hook, line, and sinker.

There is always a weaker child with twins. In this case, it was the boy. He was born with bronchitis and was prone to it throughout his short life. Tammy was average for a child her age. However, Ricky was both physically and mentally disabled. The girl advanced at a normal speed. She was running, jumping, and doing everything that was normal for a two-year-old child. But Ricky was different. although he seemed to be very smart in his own unique way.

I believe that sometimes God sends an angel into our lives for a short time so that we can see a small glimpse of what Heaven truly is. His hair was as soft as spun silk, as white as the dust of a star. When he laughed, you could not help but laugh with him. How do you hold a moonbeam in your arms?

I remember Mom would say, "If it is too quiet, they're into mischief." It never failed that she was right. It was never just one of them; everything they did, they did as a pair. They had a game where they would both hide behind the drapes. Their little hands were clasped around the drapes, as they would shake them with all their might. When you came into the room, they would start to giggle. They would laugh so hard that they would bounce on their bottoms. They knew that I was going to find them, and me grabbing them was part of the fun. One day I came in, and those little dickins pulled the drapes right down. Less than twenty minutes after they pulled down the drapes, I came into the room and caught both of them with tiny pieces of poo the size of rabbit pellets lined up in a perfect row on the coffee table. They were just so proud of themselves. How do you punish an angel? I told Mom, "I refuse to clean it up." While she cleaned up the mess, I had to leave the room. I was so close to laughing. I don't know what they had been planning to do with them. I wasn't so sure I wanted to know! Mom told me what she thought they were planning to do—but I don't even want to go there.

It took some time before I would actually notice that the boy was not developing normal. Dad mentioned that he was not catching on to feeding with a spoon. I knew that Tammy was taking her pabulum and strained food without a problem, but Ricky was not learning past the bottle. I believe that my parents thought the same as me, that the boy was possibly just behaving stubbornly. Some babies are picky eaters.

But neither could he learn to walk. I believe that my parents felt he was just going to start when he was good and ready. It was me that discovered his bad leg. He had strength in only one leg, but the other leg would just fall out from underneath him. This leg was like jelly. He could not stand on it. If he tried to stand on this leg, he would fall to the floor.

He was, in his own way, a very smart little boy. He learned on his own a very unique way of getting around. Nothing was going to hold Ricky back. He cleverly manoeuvred himself around the house by sitting on his bottom. He would put the useless leg out front, then bend his knee on the good leg so that he would have it crossed over the bad leg in front of him. He would put both hands on the floor and use them to balance himself. He would also push himself forward with his hands as he used the good leg by lifting it up and bringing it forward on the floor. Therefore, by using his good leg and both hands, he would pull himself forward. It was amazing how fast he could move. He could turn and change his direction on a dime. All this he could do while keeping his balance.

Since Ricky was always on the floor, it was not uncommon for someone to step on his fingers. When this would happen, he would not cry. Instead he would lift his hand and take a considerate look at it. For a short time, he would look concerned. He would then touch and examine the fingers, looking as though he was counting them. Once he was satisfied that his fingers were all intact, that there was no harm done, he would smile and let out a giggle. Then he would be back off on his merry way. I never recalled ever hearing him cry.

One of the things he enjoyed was rocking in our green recliner. To do this, he needed some assistance. I would pick him up and put him in the chair. Then I would sneak around the chair and rock it from behind. He would get so excited that he could make the chair rock all on his own. He would giggle the whole time the chair was rocking.

He was a very independent child. Ricky needed a sense of accomplishment. I believe that if everything had been done for him, he would have given up the will to live. "Ring Around the Rosy" was a game he got much joy out of. All of his sisters would stand in a circle and join a chain link with their hands. Because he could not stand on his own, Cathy would hold Ricky's hand on one side and I would hold his hand on the other. This would balance him so that he would not fall. Since he could not walk, we would just stand in the circle and sing the song. All the way through the lyrics, he would be smiling with excitement. When we got to all fall down, he started giggling hysterically. At this point, we would all tumble to the floor, and Ricky would come down with us.

He never learned to say more than one word. He never learned to say Mama or Dada. The only word he ever learned to say was Nana—this was the name he called me. When I came into the room, he would take one look at me and he start chattering, "Nananananananana." He would race to me as fast as he could go on that little bottom of his. If I was not in the room, he would be calling me. I went out one time for a whole day. When I got home, his eyes lit up. He started racing to get to me. When I picked him up, he was so excited that his Nana was home. Mom told me that he drove her crazy all day. She said, "He shouted for Nana from the time you left until you came in the door."

Outside of the name he called me, he spoke baby gibberish with Tammy. They both actually seemed to understand this secret language between the two of them. They spoke together in such a way that it would sound unintelligible to us. After Ricky passed away, Tammy never spoke baby gibberish again.

In November of that year, we had guests over. Mom and Dad were in the kitchen, visiting with the adults. Cathy, Sherry, and I were playing hide and seek with the children. I ran upstairs into my parents' room and hid in their large walk-in closet. To my amazement, I found a large stash of brand new toys. This was something exciting, as I had wanted a Slinky really bad... and here were three Slinkys, all brand new and still in their packages! There were toys for the twins, plus toys for us older girls. I got into the toys and shouted to the others, "Get in here and see all the toys!"

We sent three Slinkys down the steps. Mom and Dad met us at the bottom of the steps. They put all the toys away. After the guests left, Mom sat down with me and had a talk. She told me that I was now old enough to know the truth about Christmas, and that she had no intention of going back out to shop all over again. She told me that Mom and Dad always buy the gifts—and that there was no Santa Claus. Neither was there a Tooth Fairy. And no Easter Bunny, either. She said that it was all make-believe, just something parents tell their kids.

Mrs. Croft was one of our neighbours who lived in the village. She was poor. Her family lived in a shack by the tracks. She had twenty-six children and all of them shared a one-room loft. They had two king-sized beds. All the girls except for one slept in one bed while all the boys slept in the other. For a short time, the oldest girl babysat us, and most of the children went to school with us. Their mother had to teach them how to steal from the local convenience store so that they could survive. The oldest boy was funny; he was a lot of fun to have around. He was a Christian and attended the same church as we did.

My mother did fortune-telling by using ordinary playing cards. She also practiced divination, as her mother had done. All of the local neighbours would come to our house to get their fortunes read. Mrs. Croft once came to our house to have Mom read her fortune. Mom turned over the death card. She said it meant one of Mrs. Croft's children would die. Soon after, the older boy got very sick from the drinking water that they were drawing from the river. He lived six months, then he died.

One day Mrs. Croft took my parents and me up into her loft to show us the youngest child. None of us knew about this child. Neither were we prepared for what we were going to see. She brought us to the crib, which was located at the back of the loft. She had a child inside the crib. This child moved her arms and legs like a newborn infant and made the gurgling sounds of a baby. Mrs. Croft told us that she was six years old, and that mentally and physically she would never grow past this stage. She told us that for the past two years, the child had been too heavy to pick up, so now she stayed in the crib and was cared for there. My parents were horrified by what they saw. Mom looked terrified, and Dad looked shocked. They quite simply looked like they had seen the Devil himself.

My father was a descendant of Scotland, and my mother a descendant of England. We would hear about the headless horseman, and many other spooky tales that our mother had grown up with. Late one night, a dog started to howl. Mom started up about a banshee wailing, and how this meant someone was going to die. She frightened us girls. Dad told her that it was only a dog, and to shut up about it. If someone came in one door and without delay went out the other, then Mom would go into a panic. She would say, "Bad company is coming." She would break the curse by throwing salt over her right shoulder. She had a big issue with black cats, and when she pealed apples, she would let the peal drop. She would sometimes tell you your fortune, or what your future husband's name would be.

Right from the start, all this garbage had a bad effect on my life. One time, I had a most terrifying nightmare. In my dream, my little brother was running across our front lawn, when suddenly his stomach burst open and all his vital organs came spilling out. I woke up screaming. When my mother and father came in to my room, I told them, "I dreamt it. Ricky is going to die."

Mom read her own fortune. She turned over the death card, and her face went pale. She quickly got up from the table and put the cards away. Dad asked her what had spooked her. She told him that she had turned over the death card while reading her fortune. He said, "I have told you over and over again to leave the fortune-telling alone, and you never listen."

My parents had an appointment to see a paediatrician to find out why Ricky was not progressing mentally or physically. They were told that he was a Down's Syndrome child and that he would never progress past eight months old. Not one person spoke of this. It was like there was shame in the house, like a dirty word had been spoken. I was not made aware of it until after his death.

Dad once bought tickets for the Ice Capades. Everyone would be going, except for the twins. They were too young to enjoy it, so Tammy and Ricky were baby sat by Aunt Helen and Uncle Gord. This was on a Sunday. The following Monday morning started off no different than any other day. Mom and Dad got up, then Dad left for work. Normally I would have brought Ricky down to the main floor, but Mom came into the room with him in her arms. His diaper needed changing. He would need to have his bottle made and given to him. I offered to take him, and care for his needs. She turned to me and shouted, "You do not touch this child." She put him on the living room floor with no more than a wet diaper and thin t-shirt. Like always, he was cheerful. He did not fuss about the wet diaper. He lets out a giggle and then took off to play.

For two and a half years, both Mom and Dad had wanted me at home, so instead of going to school I would help care for Ricky. Now she was telling me to get out and go to school. I hesitated, then looked at him. Mom was scaring me. Something seemed seriously wrong. I was afraid of her, so I left for school. When I came in that afternoon, he was still on the floor. The urine could have been wrung out of his diaper. The diaper was almost forming icicles. I came to know that he had not eaten all day, and he had not been held. He has not been diapered or touched.

A crowded mass of snow obstructed the outside door, so that it was jammed open. It was cold in the room. The snow was blowing into the house. He sat on the floor next to the open door with no more than the thin t-shirt and diaper he'd had on that morning. Tammy was dressed extra warm and was kept away from the draft of the open door. I tried to talk to Dad, but she threatened him not to touch the child. He told me to mind my mother and do as I was told. Again she threatened me not to touch him.

For the next number of days, I watched helplessly. She would not let anyone touch him or even go near him. Dad did not try to stop her, and he did not try to help the child. Ricky developed a cold, which turned into bronchitis, developing into pneumonia. It then further developed into double pneumonia. He stayed on the floor. No one fought Mom, for the sake of the child.

Several days had now past. I came home from school and Ricky was lying limp on the floor. I begged Mom to let me pick him up. To my surprise, she did not stop me. I picked him up and sat in the rocker recliner, holding him close to me. His eyes are clouded over. I knew what death looked like. We had cats that died of distemper, so I had seen death many times. He looked into my eyes, formed his tiny lips, and whispered "Nana" for the last time. I thought he was dying. Dad came in while I was holding Ricky. I started shouting at him, "Look at his eyes! He is dying! Take him to the hospital!" He came near and looked like he was going to take the child. Then Mom shouted at him, "Don't touch that child. He will die at home." He stopped short in his tracks.

I could not believe what I was seeing. I started shouting, "Don't you care that he's dying, Daddy? Please!" He finally grabbed him out of my arms. As he ran for the door, he turned and said, "Pattie, go to your room and start praying. God answers the prayers of little girls." Although Mom protested, he would not turn back.

I got down on my knees at my bedside. This was where I pleaded with God, for what seemed like hours. I heard Dad come in. And then the television come on. But I had no intention of leaving this place of prayer. I held on to my every hope, of Ricky coming back home alive. Then the phone in the hallway rang. There was silence, then Dad called me down. He told me, "There is no more need to pray for the child. He is dead."

Mom was pounding the wall with her fists as she wailed. As I looked at her, I felt my wrath pour out. I never knew what it felt like to hate until that night. She had taken everything from me. For two and a half years, even though I was not pretty or smart, someone loved me. He loved me unconditionally, and she took him away. I turned to her as I shouted, "You killed him!"

I went to attack her. Dad grabbed me and said, "You will never tell anyone about this. You will keep your mouth shut." I went silent.

It was now March 8 and everyone was dressed for the funeral. I sat alone in the small bedroom next to the living room. Did you know that sometimes it can hurt so bad that you cannot even cry? Mom came into the room and told me that I had a visitor. A little girl about my age then came in and sat next to me on the bed. She was one of the sweetest girls I ever met. I believed that she and her family were Christians. They were very good people. It was silent for some time as she sat there beside me. Then she gave me a Raggedy Ann doll. She told me that she had made it for my birthday, but she had decided to give it to me today. I never said a word. Then she left. I don't know what happened to the doll. I never saw either it or her again. I felt so bad for how I acted that day. I never had a chance to say thank you.

I remember the tiny white casket at the head of the room. I could hear someone wailing. Then suddenly, Mom ran up to the casket and took a hold of it. She started to yank on it. It took three people to pull her off. I looked at the still lifeless body of my little brother. With all that I had within me, I was hoping that he would sit up and call my name. I wanted it to be all a bad dream, that I could wake up and find that none of this had ever happened. I thought that if I maybe wished hard enough, perhaps he would come back.

When we left the funeral home, we took most of the flowers with us. These flowers represented pain and hurt. I did not want to bring them home, but Mom and Dad overruled me. From there, we went to a house in Paris. This was where we had a small luncheon. I had never been in this house before, neither did I know the people who opened their home to us. It was nice and clean. The room was filled with the pleasant smell of sandwiches and pastries. But I did not have an appetite. Someone encouraged me to take a ham sandwich.

After the light lunch, we went home. As we traveled home, I could smell the heavy scent that came from the flowers that were in the back of the car. I could feel the warmth from the sun shining through the closed window. I looked up at the clouds and watched as their form slowly changed. It did not seem right that life could carry on like nothing had ever happened. My world had ended, and yet everything continued as before. There seemed to be no justice in this.

Mrs. Kischak, who lived in the house next to us, started to become very friendly. She had never liked my parents before, but now she was different toward them. She would encourage them to take us girls over to her home, so that they could rest. The four of us girls spent a lot of time with her. Dad commented that it took a tragedy to find out who our true friends were. There was never strife between them again.

I don't know why I did this—maybe I needed some reassurance that Ricky was in Heaven—but I went to Mom and asked, "Ricky is in Heaven with the angels, right Mom?" She turned and looked at me with anger in her face and said, "There is no God." As she spoke, it sounded more like a growl. This actually made sense to me. I walked away thinking it was like the time she had told me there was no Santa, Easter Bunny, or Tooth Fairy. Dad had told me to pray real hard, because God always answered the prayers of little girls. Well, I had prayed with every ounce of strength I had in my body, to a God I believed in. I believed that He would answer my prayer, because my dad had told me he would. Had this been another lie from adults? The pastor that I trusted had lied to me. He had lied to all the people who trusted him. Every adult I had ever trusted had lied to me. There was no Santa, no Easter Bunny, no Tooth Fairy, and now there was no God. From this, I would become an atheist. I would believe in nothing.

Now my parents would focus on Tammy. They became very concerned that she could easily die. They talked about twins being very attached to each other, and that the bond was strong. They thought she might lose the will to live, and quite simply die. This left me concerned for her as well.

I stood looking out the picture window in the living room. I don't remember what was in my head. This was when I felt a tug on my arm. Tammy was looking very intently into to my eyes. She asked me where Ricky was. At this point, I had a choice to make. Would I tell her the truth, as I knew it now, and tell her he was in the grave? That he was not coming back? That he was dead? Or would I lie like everyone else has done to me, and tell her what I once believed? If I told her the truth, as I knew it now, would she give up the will to live and then also die?

I kneeled before her, cupped her tiny face into my hands, and said, "Ricky is in Heaven with the angels." I thought, *What have I got to fear if I tell a lie? Is there a God in Heaven to punish me?* Then she asked if he was coming back. I answered, "He cannot come back to us, but someday we will be with him in Heaven." I no longer had the faith to believe what I had told her, but I was comfortable with the thought that this would be enough to keep her from giving up the will to live. The answer I gave her must have been enough, because she never came back with any more questions. I was so relieved that she came to me, and not our mother. The answer my mother had given me would have crushed her.

Throughout the last week of Ricky's life, he never once received a bottle or any kind of liquid, and of course the bottle was his only means of nourishment. I tried to help him, and Mom went after me with a broom handle. Now it was just her and I alone in the house. Dad was gone to work and there was no one here to protect her. I grabbed the broom handle and started coming after her. Tammy started to cry. When I saw that I was scaring my baby sister, I backed off and put the weapon down.

I was full of vengeance and anger toward my mother. Today violence is running rampant on the television. Kids are exposed to violence that children in the 60s were totally clueless about. If ever I had been exposed to all the violence today's kids are influenced by, I know I would have stabbed my mother in the night, multiple times, with a butcher knife—and maybe my father as well. When I think of it, Dad always had a loaded rifle in the house. This might sound outrageous, but I am telling the truth. I was hurting and could not find it in me to forgive her, and quite simply my father was just as much at blame for my brother's death as she was.

I woke from my sleep, hearing Ricky calling out, "Nana, Nana." That was when I got out of my bed and went into my mother and father's bedroom, where his crib was still up. I was half awake, and I thought he was calling me. As I came around the corner, I saw that he was not there. Then I remembered that he was dead. I took hold of the crib railing and wailed loudly. I slid down to the floor, waking up Dad and Mom. It took both of them to pry me away from the crib. My grip on the rails was so tight that my knuckles were white.

I knew the next morning what my parents planned to do. There was no way they were doing it. Dad said that the crib, and all Ricky's stuff, had to come down.

There was a large NHL picture on the back of the cereal box. On the front was a colourful rooster and the name of the brand of cereal—Corn Flakes. Every time Dad bought Corn Flakes, it would be a different NHL player. Simple things like this gave Ricky joy. I would cut every one of the pictures out for him and would tape them to the wall and ceiling surrounding his crib, so that he could get pleasure from them. Every time he went into his crib, as he looked at his pictures, he would start to giggle. I had six of these pictures up for him. I would pin up his pictures while he watched, and you could see the joy in his eyes as I was doing this. He also had a stuffed black dolphin that was soft, just like a pillow. It was the same size as him. When I put him to bed at night, I would give him his dolphin. He would snuggle with it. If anyone else dared to put him to bed, he would put up a fuss.

My parents had plans of taking down everything. There was an opened trunk in the corner of their bedroom. They planned to put some of his things into the trunk. Among these things would be his hockey pictures, but they were going to throw out his dolphin and give away his crib. I pleaded with them not to take anything down, but they only ignored me. I was not ready for his belongings to come down. They did decide to keep the dolphin, but it was put away along with everything else. The crib was given away. It seemed to me they found it easy to dispose of a child they did not want. And it was not difficult for them to get rid of everything that was a reminder there had ever been a little boy named Ricky who lived in this house. There were a couple of times when my father mentioned that the coroner had said Ricky's stomach had been totally empty except for a small jelly-like substance. The coroner thought he might have been poisoned. When Dad mentioned this, Mom was very quiet. He tried to put the blame on Aunt Helen and Uncle Gord, because they'd had him on the Sunday when we went to the Ice Capades. But I knew that Mom had been alone with him. So if anyone poisoned him, it would have been my mother.

Why does the sun keep on shining?
Why does the sea rush to shore?
Don't they know it is the end of the world?
It ended when he said goodbye.[1]

---

[1] Skeeter, Davis. "The End of the World." *Skeeter Davis Sings The End of the World*. RCA Victor, 1963.

# CHAPTER 4

# IT IS IN SILENCE THAT I WEEP

*A*s a young child, I felt we would always live on the farm in Canning. To this day, I still believe that had Ricky lived, my parents would have grown old on the farm. It is my belief that they could no longer live with all the memories that haunted them in that house, so they sold the farm to a doctor and bought a house in Paris. I did not want to leave. For me, it just seemed that we were drifting further and further apart from all the material things that kept his memory alive in me.

It was many years after my brother's death before I saw my mother read cards again. She replaced card-reading with Ouija boards and magnetic righting. She also became a heavy drinker. She would hide her bottles under her bed and drink anything that had alcohol in it. I never recalled seeing her drink before this, although I knew about their drinking parties. Before the death of my brother, it was actually my dad who I had seen drunk.

My mother also became a chain smoker. She was on a desperate mission to call back the dead. It was almost like the cigarettes were the very fuel that fed her. My mother's one hand was continually grasping at her cigarette. She would take a quick puff, then quickly her hands would be back on the Ouija board, searching desperately for the child she longed to make amends with. When she was not doing this, she was in the hotel bar feeding herself with the only thing that could dull her senses. Then perhaps she could forget the dreadful truth that so greatly hunted her.

The death of my brother did not seem to have a large effect on the three younger girls. To my relief, Tammy seemed to bounce back immediately from this terrible ordeal. Cathy and Sherry did not seem to be affected at all. My dad lost his will to joke around, which must have been a relief to my mother, as she had found his odd sense of humour very repulsive. He actually became very serious, turning into the sensible one out of the two. But I looked at him as a worthless coward who did not have the backbone to stand up against his wife. Instead he let her slowly and cruelly take the life of their only son. I found myself having pity on him. I was so young that I desperately needed a parent I could count on. I quickly found myself turning to my father for my mentor. Truly, I had no one else to turn to.

Following the death of my brother, I stopped talking. I would still speak the odd word or two, but only if I was pressured to do so. Of course, now that Ricky was gone there was no purpose in me staying home, so I went back to school, as I had done before the birth of the twins. Because of my appearance and the fact that I could neither learn nor talk, it was acknowledged by all that I was retarded. This would result in students, teachers, my father, and even strangers verbally and physically abusing me.

My dad tried to make the best of our first Christmas without Ricky. He bought outdoor lights for the front of our home. He strung a string of amber lights across the front of the house and he installed green, blue, and red floodlights to glow against the snow-covered bushes. I made a gold-coloured wreath at school. Dad hung my wreath on our front door. I had to admit that we did have the most lovely decorated home on that street. Dad came home from work, and as he walked in the door he commented on how nice the lights looked out front.

Dad came in from work early that Christmas Eve. It was somewere around 3:00 p.m. that he staggered in. I met him at the door as he entered the house. I had only seen him drunk like this one other time, and it was when I was so young that I could hardly remember it. But never had I seen him like this. He told me that he did not want me to see him in this condition. I could tell he was having a lot of trouble standing up, so I followed him down to the laundry room. He took hold of the tub and cried out, "Help me, Pattie, the room is spinning." And then he barfed in the laundry tub.

He spent some time down in the basement. I went back upstairs and sat at the kitchen table with my three sisters, expecting that Mom was going to make a decent Christmas Eve dinner. She came in the room, opened the freezer door, and tossed four frozen meat pies on the table. She said, "I am going to the hotel. This is your dinner." I was staring at the frozen meat pies in total disbelief.

That was when Dad came in. He asked, "What is this?" I explained to him what she'd done, to which he said, "I guess I will have to stay sober for the sake of my children." I never saw him drunk again after that.

It was somewhere in this timeframe that Grampa Campbell died. There was so much stress going on that I am not sure whether my dad even focused on the loss of his father. All I can recall of his death was that the coffin was made of hardwood— and it was large, on account that Grampa was a tall man.

The spirit that spoke to Mom through the Ouija board suggested to her that if she wanted to communicate directly with Ricky, she would have to take the next step and go on to magnetic righting. This spirit then taught her how to do the righting. Mom and Dad both considered that I took Ricky's death much harder than they did. Therefore, when my mother discovered that she was communicating with a spirit that called itself Ricky, she right away called me into the room to share her joy with me. She showed me the magnetic righting and how it was done. The spirit told her that it did not want to talk to me, just her. Something did not seem to add up here, therefore it did not bother me in the slightest bit that whatever this was did not want to speak with me.

The spirit that called itself Ricky told Mom that what she had done was dreadful, but that she could make things right between him and her by doing what he told her to do. He told her to start bringing home fallen angels, and that she would find them at the hotel. He told her that when she brought them home, she had to please them by entertaining them. Whatever they wanted, she was to do it for them. Mom sat me down in her bedroom and explained all this to me. She would bring men home every night. I don't know what they were doing. Mom wanted me to stay in my bed when these men were in the house.

When she got into the magnetic righting, strange things started happening. I had a pair of gold fish in my bedroom. My father's woman friend was living in a room in our finished basement. She had a cat that had free run of our home. I was concerned that the cat could kill and eat my fish, and therefore I kept my fish bowl on the dresser inside of my grandmother's old bird cage. I hoped this would make it impossible for the cat to get to my fish. I also had a full bottle of nail polish remover in my dresser, which only I knew was there.

I was awakened one night to a loud crash. My grandmother's bird cage had come crashing to the floor. All over the floor was broken glass from the cage, but the fish bowl remained untouched. The foot of my bed was wet with nail polish remover. Dad and his girlfriend, Grace, were the first to come in. They had been sleeping in the spare bedroom in the basement. After they came in, my mother entered my room. Therefore, there was no way that anyone else could have been in my room when this happened. In the presence of all three witnesses, I brought out my nail polish remover bottle, which was still in my dresser where I had put it the night before. It had been emptied.

One night, one of my mother's fallen angels misunderstood which door led to the bathroom. He opened my bedroom door and came in. Like any twelve-year-old girl, I grabbed my blankets and pulled them up to my throat. I started screaming. No matter how hard he tried to apologize for his misjudgement, I kept screaming until Dad finally came to my aid. My father kicked Mom's friend out. Mom's fallen angel must have thought both of my parents had a few screws loose.

Of course, Dad had been downstairs with his girlfriend, Grace. This woman had no intention of staying in the basement. I believe she was watching for the perfect chance to take over. I had no idea how wicked she was. After this incident with the fallen angel, Grace decided that she was going to take over the house by getting rid of my mother. She would entice me to torment my mother. I was so full of vengeance towards Mom that it did not take much to encourage the type of behaviour Grace was hoping for. And no one was telling me not to attack her. Therefore, I started tormenting my mother.

Mom remained peaceful, however. This was not working out for Grace. So again she told me to try harder. I was so full of hatred that of course Grace was only fuelling the fire. I went after her again. This time my mother experienced what looked like a nervous breakdown. She started leaping around and freaking out. This was what Grace wanted. She went to Dad and suggested that since my mother was mentally challenged, he should put her away. And that was what he did. I had no idea what I was getting myself into. I was out of the frying pan and right into the fire. This would be the beginning of three years of relentless torment from a woman who had no mercy for her victims. I could not blame anyone but myself for the misery I was about to experience.

Grace was overbearing. Through fear, she would manipulate and control. She was a large woman and she would manipulate her victims by pushing her weight around. You could see it in his face that Dad was terrified of her. He would not fight her. She got everything she wanted by terrorizing him. That included inflicting pain upon me—both emotional and physical. She tossed out all of his mother's Christmas ornaments, both the tiny red heart that had such a special place in my heart and Dad's angel, the one he wanted hung on the tree every year.

When we moved into town, Dad had bought me a bedspread and drapes for my bedroom. She took that from me, saying that I was too young to appreciate something like that. She hung my drapes in her and Dad's room. He had given them to me, but he would not say a word in my defence. She would use the flyswatter on my bottom. I don't remember this, but I know it happened. One day while I was babysitting Tammy, I was expected to give her a bath. Tammy was fighting me and I was terrified of what Grace would do to me if I failed to bathe her. The stress was badly built up in me, so I took the flyswatter and used it on her wet bare bottom. It left red welts on her. When Dad and Grace saw it, I was scolded. They showed me what I did. I asked, "If it leaves a mark like that, then why would an adult do it to a child?" Dad told me, "I have never done that to you, or any of your sisters. Nether has your mother." That was when he looked at Grace, and fear filled his faced. After he left the room, she told me that I was going to get it for that.

I never remembered the actual beatings. Many years later, Cathy told me that she had been beating me. She would have my sister stand and watch. Most likely, this was intended to threaten Cathy, as though to say, "If you anger me, this is what you will get." Again I saw my dad as a worthless wimp.

I met a very nice boy in Paris. His father was friends with my dad. Both of them worked together at the Ford plant in Oakville. They would carpool back and forth to work. In spite of all my physical and emotional problems, this boy liked me for who I was. I would not talk very much, but he told me he liked me that way. He was a real chatterbox, so we were great together. He did all the talking, and I did all the listening. He told me that he was going to marry me someday. I really enjoyed his company as well.

I was going through a lot of emotional and physical abuse in the school, not just from the students but the teachers as well. There was one particular boy in my Special Education class who had it out for me. I was terrified of him and was trying to avoid him as much as possible. One day the boy from school saw me holding hands with my boyfriend. The next time he saw me at school, he told me he knew now why I was trying to avoid him. I just looked at him without speaking a word. He got angry and told me that he would put an end to me and my boyfriend.

He later told my boyfriend that I did with him a thing you would only do if you were married. When my boyfriend confronted me on what the other boy had said, I told him that it was not true and that I did not understand what he was talking about. My boyfriend was a Christian boy, so he was very angry. He said that there was no way I could not know anything about sex. Therefore, he broke up our friendship. He was a very special guy. He never once tried to make me do anything a good girl would not want to do. I really missed him for a long time after that.

All I had to do was walk home from school and the local students from the Catholic school would start shouting, "She is ugly enough that she should be stoned." They would chase me with baseball bats and start throwing stones at me. I was terrified to walk out of the house. My young boyfriend was no longer my friend, and I was afraid to go out anywhere by myself. If I walked uptown, people would point across the street at me and say, "Look how ugly she is. She must be retarded."

At home, I was getting the same thing. My sister Cathy was the only one who stuck close to me throughout my whole childhood. When you lose someone through death, you go through stages. I had yet to come to the reality that Ricky was not going to come back from the dead. It took me two years before I came to that stage in my life. Only then could I even start to begin life again.

One afternoon, I was sitting quietly on the sofa in the living room. I suddenly became aware that Ricky was never coming back. For two years I had barely said a word, as I ached silently inside my heart for the loss of my dear brother. Right there, in the silence of the room, I knew he would never come back. I started to wail at the very top of my lungs. I grasped my head in my hands as I rocked back and forth on the sofa. My head was pounding. Dad and Grace came into the room. One of them asked me what was wrong. I started to cry out, "He is not coming back." Grace asked, "Who is not coming back?" I wailed, "Ricky is not coming back." Dad told Grace that I had taken Ricky's death harder than anyone else had.

They left the room for a short minute. You would expect that they may come back with some Tylenol, or perhaps hug me. But no, not my father. He came back around the corner and told me, "Your mother was unfaithful to me. She had an Italian boyfriend who she was sleeping with when she got pregnant with you. I am stuck with you because she is in a mental hospital and not capable of caring for you. I don't want you. You remind me of your mother's unfaithfulness. Grace and I were involved a year before you were conceived. Grace's daughter is my child, you are not. I would rather have her daughter living here than to have you. You are only here because I am stuck with you. If I had a choice, you would not be in this house. I have never loved you, and I don't love you now. Your mother does not love you either. She tried to kill you before you were born. You're not pretty or smart enough to be my child. Only attractive children are born into the Campbell family."

I saw Grace looking around the corner at me. She had a smug grin on her face as she glared. When she saw that I had caught her watching, she backed into the hall. With sarcasm, I thought,

*Thank you, Dad. What perfect timing.* I got up and took something for my throbbing headache.

During this time, there was an angel of a girl who came into my life for a short time. She was pretty enough that I was surprised she wanted to hang out around me. One day while I was passing the Catholic school, a group of boys came after me with their bats and stones. This girl came running out into their midst shouting, "Don't touch her." She walked me home that day. After that, she would come and meet me every day at my home. She always had some kind of pleasant thing planned for us to do.

One day, we simply went out and picked lilacs. She told me that she did not like Grace, that Grace gave her bad vibes. I really liked her and felt safe when she was with me. When she was there, no one tried to harm me. She tried to get me to talk, but no matter her effort, I was silent. When three days had past and she had not come to the house, I wondered what might have happened. As much as I feared going out on my own, I went over to her house to check on her. She stepped outside of the house and told me that she had received a very bad walloping on account of me. She told me that her brother had told her dad about the kindness she was showing to me, and that her father wanted her to stay away from me. She got a thrashing just for spending time with me.

I stood in silence as she told me everything. Then she said, "Why do I even bother to talk to you? You never speak." She started to head for the door as she told me that she would never bother with me again. That was when I spoke up, saying, "I am sorry that you got punished on account of me. You did not deserve it. You are a very kind person." She turned and looked at me. This was the first time she had ever heard my voice. She still looked bitter as she walked into the house. She never came back to my home again. I thought that maybe her Dad did not like the name Campbell. There were a lot of people who did not seem to like me because of my name. Or maybe it was because she was

Catholic, and I was Protestant. Or quite possibly, it might have been because everyone thought I was retarded. And of course, I was ugly.

Dad wanted to know what happened to my friend. Grace said that I was too ugly to have a pretty friend like that. She said the girl quit coming over because I was ugly, but I knew the truth.

There was only one time that Dad took us girls to see our mother. She was now out of the hospital. Mom was living in a small apartment in Brantford. There were very small windows. It was dark and dreary. She had favoured Tammy from birth, even more so since Ricky's death. She paid no attention to the rest of us girls. She only seemed to be interested in Tammy. I did not really care whether we went back again.

I had done good at babysitting for my sisters and brother, therefore a good word had been circulated about me. On account of this, I was receiving a great deal of babysitting jobs for people in Paris and the surrounding area. Two years in a row, I made enough money to cover all my school supplies as well as my back-to-school clothes.

One night, I was to babysit for a family that lived in Brantford. They had heard about my brother's illness and how I had cared for him. They had a three-month-old baby, and they wanted someone who would be responsible enough to care for it. They had my dad take me to their home in Brantford so that I could sit for them. I had a very bad feeling as I was coming in the house. I asked Dad if he would pick me up and bring me home that night. He refused to do that. He told me it was too far to drive. He wanted me to stay the night. They had three boys, plus the small baby. I stayed up as late as I could keep my eyes open. I was afraid to go to bed. I felt something bad was going to happen to me.

It was 11:00 at night when I fell to sleep. They wanted me in the spare bedroom that was connected to their room, because the baby slept in their bedroom with them. This kept me close to the baby. I woke up through the night to a man trying to force himself inside of me. I had no idea what sex was, but something inside of me said this was not good. I fought the man off and I tried to hide in the closet. He pulled the closet door open. He was pulling me out of the closet when the baby started crying for its feeding. He left through the door, where his wife asked what he had been doing in the room I was sleeping in. It was so dark in the room that I never did see the man's face.

Dad picked me up the next morning. I was very shook up. After we left the house, I told Dad what he had done to me. Grace was in the car with us. We went back to the house with a police officer. I told the officer what had been done to me. The wife told the officer that her husband had been in their room with her the whole night and that they had no idea what I was talking about. The husband's brother was sleeping on the sofa. Therefore, the police told Dad and Grace that there was too much confusion about what had happened. Therefore, there was not a thing they could do about it.

Grace started coming down on me very hard about modest dressing. She had me in skirts that hung between my ankles and knees. I had to wear long-sleeved white blouses that buttoned to my neck. To make this dress code even worse, there was embroidery on the collar of every blouse. She may have liked the embroidery, but I was the one wearing it—and I was the one being made fun of. None of the other youth dressed like this. She wanted my body to be fully covered. It was at this time that Dad sold the house in Paris. He bought a two hundred acre farm in Nile, a small village located nine miles north of Goderich, Ontario.

# CHAPTER 5

# GABLE IN MY ROOM

*W*e traveled over three hundred miles the day we moved. My father drove our car while Uncle Gord drove the moving van. The four of us girls traveled with Dad and Grace. The farm was located on a dirt road. The house had a white frame with black trim. Just to the left of the house was the barn and barnyard. We entered the house on the left side. The entry was a small closed-in porch. Right across from the entry was the door that led into a large country-style kitchen. Behind the kitchen was a large shed that was connected to the house. Half of it had a raised-plank floor. That was where our well was located. The other half was a dirt floor. The living room was at the front of the house. There was a small bedroom next to the living room. That would be my father and Grace's room. The three-piece bath was also on the main floor. There were two bedrooms on the second floor.

Grace walked through the house with me. I could not figure out what was up with her. She was behaving extra nice with me. Therefore, I did not trust her. I kept my guard up. Entering the second level, we went into the bedroom that was located at the back of the house. When we got into this room, I noticed right away the gable that overlooked the barn and barn yard. Grace must have seen the gleam in my eyes. She told Dad, "Pattie gets this room. She likes the gable." I could not figure out what was up with her, but I did like the bedroom, and the gable really appealed to me. So that was fine with me.

Later, when she was unpacking the boxes, she took her daughter's picture out of the frame she had it in and put my picture in the frame in its place. She said that I was now her special girl. All along I was thinking, *What is she trying to prove here?*

Every time I would start a new school, I would find myself hoping that with a new beginning I could somehow wake up and be a genius. Like all children, I had dreams. I knew when I was finished school what I wanted to be. I never dared tell anyone what my wishes were, though; I knew I would be made fun of. My dreams were only dreams. Many little girls want to be models. Some little boys want to be firemen. I wanted to be a judge of the Supreme Courts of Canada. I knew if ever I could learn the way I wanted to, then there would be no end to what I could do with my life. I did not want to babysit for the rest of my life, and I did not want to be dependent on a man, or anyone else. But my future looked very dismal. My desire was to be successful, no matter how hard I had to work. My best was all I could give, but it was not enough.

Starting school in Nile would prove to be the most difficult hurtle I would ever have to cross. I found farm kids to be very arrogant in a cruel, ruthless way. I am sure the dress code that Grace had me wearing was not helping the matter in the slightest. Once again my deformities, mental slowness, and lack of being able to communicate were setbacks for me. I made the odd friend here and there, but most of the students treated me as if I was inferior to them.

We did not grow up in a clean house, neither were we taught to bathe. Plus I worked in the barn with my dad, meaning there would be an unpleasant odour hovering around me. I was made fun for this as well. Quite simply, if you have lived in that type of lifestyle from as far back as you can remember, you will not notice the bad odour that is coming from you.

By this time, I knew school was a lost cause. My hope of succeeding through the school system was not going to happen. It did not take long before the teachers became aware of my talent with sketching, however. One of the teachers wanted a mural done. There was a certain group of girls that had been assigned every year to do the mural. I was promised a good grade for this assignment. The girls who would have otherwise done it became very bitter. As far as receiving a good grade went, it would never be enough to benefit me for the future. For the sake of making it easier for myself with those who considered themselves superior to me, I took it on myself to make a mess out of the mural. When the girls saw it, they started belittling me. I asked the girls why they would think that I could not draw better than that. I told them, "Go to the teacher, show her the mess I made, and she will assign it to you. Take the assignment that you wanted." I had hoped I would be treated a little better for my unselfish act, but I did not even get a thank you. The girls went to the teacher and showed her my poor artwork. Then they took over the assignment. They didn't treat me any different afterwards.

One day, my sisters and I were heading home on the school bus when another child said something along the lines that Grace was my mother. I was very offended by this remark. Although I seldom spoke, this time I turned and looked the child right in the face, and said, "She is not my mother." One of my sisters ran into the house and informed Grace what I had said. Cathy told me years later that it was the worst beating she ever gave me. Of course, I have no memory of it.

When Grace wanted to get rid of people who were a burden on her, she would have them put away. After this episode on the bus, she decided that I had to go. She may have been thinking that I could be a threat to her, that she could be kicked out. She set an appointment with a psychiatrist. She knew my weaknesses.

She talked with him. She told him what questions she wanted him to ask me. By the time he was finished with me, I felt like a degenerate idiot. He told Grace that I should be put away in a home for the mentally challenged. Fortunately, Dad finally did protest, so nothing came of her plan.

Grace's mother was a kind woman. She seemed to have an act with kids. Grace's daughter Linda refused to live with her mother, so she lived with her Gram. I could fully understand why Linda felt this way. It amazed me that Grace even came from the same bloodline as her mother. This was not a case of mother like daughter. Gram was a refuge. She was like a cold cup of water to a dry and parched land. At this time, I needed all the comfort I could get.

During the summer holidays, Gram took Cathy and me for two weeks. She had our visit fully planned. Because Linda was popular, at first I was afraid of her. It was always the popular ones who treated me bad, but Linda was not like that and neither were her friends. Linda was included in all the plans Gram made for us. First of all, she took the three of us out shopping for clothes. Linda helped Cathy and I choose a skirt and shirt that were fashionable with the teen trend. It had been a long time since I had worn a short skirt, and these were miniskirts.

We went to a beach party with Linda and her friends. There was a dance with a live band. It was very wild compared to what I was used to. The youth were kissing and touching on the dance floor and at their tables. Some would couple together and leave, then later return. Linda did this as well. I was not comfortable with my surroundings, therefore Cathy and I just stayed in the crowded area. There were a couple of rapes that happened on the beach that night, so I was glad that we had made a wise choice by staying in the dance hall.

Gram lived above the stores in the downtown section of Brantford. She was on the second floor. Below her apartment was the cement sidewalk and paved street. The nights were hot and sticky. Therefore, she had the window open in the room where Cathy and I slept. There was no screen in the window, and the window sill was wide enough that a child could easily lie down on it.

Cathy would sleepwalk. I woke one night and saw her lying on the windowsill, sound asleep. I was afraid if I tried to move her, I could startle her and she would land on the pavement below. I went into Gram's bedroom and told her that my sister was sleeping on the sill. She came in and carefully picked Cathy up. Then she put her sleeping body safely back in the bed.

Gram and Linda told me how pleased they were that I had overcome my fear enough to speak up. The last night we stayed there, Gram put on a party for Linda, me, and my sister. Gram chaperoned from the other room, so it was just like a grown-up party. This way she also showed us that she trusted us. I was very afraid of Linda's friends, therefore I appreciated the fact that Gram was just over in the other room. Linda and her friends told me that they liked me, that I was a really great person and that they appreciated the fact that I did not tell how bad the beach party really was. All considered, I had a great time at Gram's.

Grace would work on a person's nerves until she gave them a nervous breakdown. I had taken all I could handle. There was no way I could go back to that. Dad returned for us the following afternoon. On the way home, I told him to pull over and let me out of the car. He asked why. I told him that I would not go back to the house as long as that woman was there. Then again I told him, "Pull over and let me out. If you take me back as it is now, I will pack my bags and leave tonight." He promised me that when we got home she would leave.

Stepping in the door, Dad picked up the phone receiver, dialled a number, and handed the receiver to Grace. He told her to get a ride out, for she was leaving that night. The next day, Mom was home. The only thing I felt bad about was the fact that

Grace would have gone home to her mother and daughter. Linda was a nice girl; she did not deserve that.

As much as I should have been grateful for the fact that Grace was gone, as soon as I set my eyes on my mother, the vengeful anger flared back up. Quite simply, I still could not forgive her for the death of my brother. If I had learned anything from Grace, it was how to make people's lives unbearable. Now that my mother was back in the house, I started tormenting her all over again. I would entice Cathy to join me in bullying our mother. My sister thought it was just a game, but I was fully aware of my actions.

Spiritual chaos started happening as soon as my mother was back in our home. Cast-iron frying pans started lifting off the surface of the stove, then floating across the room, then dropping to the floor. Coffee mugs would do the same. Most of the time, these objects would come within inches of hitting either Cathy or me.

One day, as I came into the kitchen, I saw something that gripped me with fear. My mother looked like she was in a trance. As she walked across the floor, she would open the cupboard drawers and pull out the carving knifes. She was running her fingers over the sharp blade of the knives. She stared blankly into space as she did this. Suddenly, the death of my brother flashed through my head. All I could think was that I had to get my sisters out of the house as fast as I could. It did not matter that anything could happen to me. My fear was for what she could do to my younger sisters.

I told Cathy to grab Sherry and run for the door. I said, "Don't look back. Just keep running." I grabbed Tammy and took off for the door as fast as I could. I heard Mom shouting, "Bring those children back." But I kept shouting ahead for the girls to run and not look back. We did not go back to the house until I saw from our hiding place that Dad was home.

Within days of Grace moving out, our neighbour, who rented a barn and house off of my father, invited Cathy and I into her home to teach us how to do a blind hem on a skirt. She sat both of us down at her table and taught us. I remember that my skirt was pink. The next day we wore our skirts to school. My experience had so far been that no boy found me appealing to any degree. And after the experience I had babysitting in Brantford, I did not care to have a man or boy near me.

Getting on to the bus that morning was the most unpleasant experience I could have had. Between my fear of other students and being a very shy person, this was not an ideal situation for me. I expected to hear, "Oh, she stinks, she's ugly," and all the other cruel remarks that were commonly thrown my way when I entered the bus. But this I did not expect. As I entered the bus and started down the rows of seats, the boys started howling like wolves. I could also hear someone thumping their foot on the floor. I sat down and stared straight ahead, paying no attention to anyone on the bus. I hoped this would shut them up. I could hear them remarking about my legs.

Ken Macintosh was a boy who seemed to carry a large chip on his shoulder. He always had a miserable look on his face, and he made me very uncomfortable. The older boys were poking fun of Ken for staring at my legs. He got offensive and told them to shout up. I could hear someone remarking that they wanted to touch my legs. That made me feel very uncomfortable.

It was this morning on the bus that I found out a certain young girl was giving herself to the boys in a very inappropriate way. She was very angry that I was getting all this attention— attention that, of course, I did not want. Before that day was over, I found out that one of our custodians should have never been hired by the school board. The way he was staring at me was giving me the creeps.

I feared Ken with good reason. I would get a bad feeling around him. Today I acknowledge that what made me uneasy about him was bad spirits. He went to a girl that lived in the same village as I. He bargained with her to set me up so that I would be alone with him and another older boy who lived in the village, whose name was Sam. Between Ken and Sam, they wanted me alone for the intention of raping me. She knew that I was not popular. They told her that it was an initiation, to formally initiate me into the popular group. When she gave me their invitation, she told me that I was to meet them in an old, deserted barn. I asked her who I was to meet, and she told me it was Ken and his friend Sam.

As soon as she said Ken's name, I felt the hair on the back of my neck go up. I said no. She tried to tell me that if I wanted to be popular, I had to do this. Again I made my feelings clear: "No, I will not be alone with him. I don't trust him." She took the message back. When she came back to me, she told me that I was wise in not trusting him. They had got angry at her for messing up and told her they had intended to rape me. That day, she and I became friends. They did try more than just the one time to get themselves alone with me, but all their efforts failed.

Although she was getting up in years, we still had the dog that my dad had picked up at the auction sales barn so many years before. Sandy's hearing and eyesight was gone, but she had a good sense of danger. She was more like a friend than a dog. She had been an excellent herding dog. There was no person or animal she could not round up.

One evening, as it was nearing midnight, Cathy and I went out walking. Because Sandy's sight and hearing were poor, for her safety we closed her in the house. As we entered into the village, Ken and Sam saw that we were alone. Somehow they put some distance between Cathy and me so that they could start to circle around me, in case I tried to run. They would have grabbed me, so that was no option. As they walked around me, they closed in. They did it as though they were rounding up livestock. I had the good sense to know that what they intended to do was the same as that man who had tried to rape me while I was babysitting. Therefore, I was terrified. Suddenly Cathy said, "Pattie, look!

Sandy is circling around them, and closing in on them, just as they are doing to you." When they turned and looked at Sandy, they took off running.

If there was anything that I longed for, it was to again hear the sweet tender voice of my little brother calling out Nana. I told my new friend how much I missed him and how much I longed to hear his voice again. I don't recall whether it was her idea or mine, but we devised the plan together that I would lead in a séance to call my little brother back from the dead. Cathy was terrified. She would have nothing to do with what we were up to. Mom was the one who surprised me, though. With all the witchcraft she was involved in, I would have thought a séance would not bother her. But she did not want anything to do with it. Therefore it was only Pam and I that participated in this action.

We lit a candle in the center of the kitchen table. Then she sat in a chair across from me. We held hands in a circle around the candle. Then we started to call on Ricky. The Devil is not a gentleman. If you open the door for him, he will come in. After he enters through the open door, the only possible way to get rid of him is through the power of the Holy Spirit of God. I saw in the corner of the kitchen a white glow. Pam did not see it. The spirit moved towards me. When it came to me, it gave the illusion that my chair was rolling back and forth. That was when it all came to a stop.

After that night, Cathy started having nightmares. She said that a spirit was telling her that because she disliked it, the spirit did not like her. She had to go on sleeping pills so that she could sleep. I did not know it then, but I know now that it was my séance that started the trouble.

During my last year of public school, the class that Cathy and I attended did a student exchange. My sister and I shared our student. She was a black girl named Sasha who lived in Chicago, Illinois. The word was quickly spread throughout the town of Goderich that there would be black children visiting in various homes throughout the surrounding region. This would be the first time that I would hear the common slang term for a Negro person. I had always kept my hurt deep inside of me, and never spoke of my feelings. Therefore, I was going to be surprised at my reaction when I heard someone mistreating another, simply because their skin was black. No one had ever told me this name was an unkind thing to call a black person; it was in the tone that they said it.

The first time I heard this inconsiderate name calling, I lost my temper. I told the person what I thought of their ignorance. People in the Goderich region were speaking of these people in this tone even before they set foot on our doorsteps. It must have been all the hurt that had been building up from as far back as I could recall, but I could not take someone inflicting pain on another. Seeing such actions brought out of me a tremendous anger. I believe that Cathy did not understand the meaning of this disgraceful word, but when my sister used it to refer to Sasha, I blew up at her and again told Cathy just what I thought of her actions.

I was concerned that my actions could have been mistaken for being arrogant, but that would have not been at all true. I knew that the families lodging the other children were not acting hospitable towards them, because after they had been chatting in private with Sasha she told me that her friends wished they could have stayed with us. I found myself being very protective of her. My dad was in the habit of trying to grab our teenage friends in a sexually provocative way, so I was also glad that he never tried to touch Sasha.

Now it was our turn to visit the exchange students. There was only supposed to be one child per student, but again I was allowed to go. I was about to have an experience that I would never forget. I had never heard the word "love" before, plus I had no idea what that word even meant. Since my Aunt Norma, there had been no one who cuddled me. Therefore, I had not received affection from anyone in a long time. I had received plenty of verbal and physical abuse, but that was the extent of it.

For two weeks, we lodged in the black section of Chicago. Entering their home, I was welcomed warmly by Sasha's family. The first night in their home, her mother gave both Cathy and me a sponge bath. Although I was fourteen, I did not argue the point. Instead I was submissive to her. She had been very kind to me, and I had no reason to fear her. She fully bathed me, and then dressed me in my pyjamas. She did it in a gentle way. She showed me only kindness. She was amazed when I did not speak, even to protest against the sponge bath. After she was finished, she told me to bathe every night in the same manner as she had done. I felt embarrassed that she had bathed me, but my difficulties at speaking kept me from protesting. So as to avoid going through this again, I did as she told me.

Sasha's relatives, and friends of their family, came in to visit while we were there. Everyone was thrilled to meet me. They told me that when Sasha came home from the student exchange, she had said kind things about me. Everyone thanked me for giving her nothing but kindness, all the time while she had stayed in our home.

Sasha's mother told Cathy and me that they lived in a very dangerous section of the city. Their home was an apartment above the stores in the down town section of Chicago. Although she told us that it was not safe to go out after dark, there was one night when we did go out. Since she had an appointment that night, we went to the hair salon. From there, we went to the church their family attended. Although I was not in the habit of going to church anymore, I was polite and did not protest. No one was cruel or rude with me—not even the ruffians on the street. Not one person said I was ugly or retarded.

Right away, I noticed that these people treated me in a very kind way. If they had nothing to say to me, they were polite enough not to say anything at all. Automatically I found myself liking them. I liked the thugs as well, since they didn't have anything cruel to say about my appearance, either. The point was this—everyone treated me with respect.

Church was an experience that I would never forget as long as I live. It did not take long before I knew that this was nothing like the little church I had attended in Canning. I sat quietly as I watched everyone pray and worship. Next thing I noticed was that they were all speaking in a foreign tongue that I had never heard before. That was when every person in the church started to cry. Although I no longer believed in God, I could tell that these people knew how to pray. But what astonished me even more was this comfortable feeling that I got. I had this same feeling all the time while I was in their house, but in the church it felt even stronger. I recognized the feeling from when I would hold and play with my brother. I could not deny that I liked the feeling. I did not know what love felt like, so there was no way for me to understand what this feeling was.

Although I found that the Negro people ate pretty much the same food as we did, there was one evening when we sat down to dinner and Sasha's mother served cornmeal bread. Our dinner was placed on our plate, and then we were expected to eat. As soon as I tasted the cornmeal bread, I did not like it. I was nervous that I would be expected to eat everything that was on my plate. I boldly spoke up and said, "I don't like the bread." I expected to be corrected, as Grace had done, but Sasha's mom did something totally out of the normal. With excitement, she exclaimed, "She spoke! Pattie has not said a word since she came here." She did not scold me, nor did she make me eat the bread.

For the remainder of the time we were there, she tried to get me to talk, but I never did say another word. The last night we were there, she sat in bed with me and cuddled me for some time while she rocked me in her arms. When she left the room, I could overhear her speaking with her husband. She said that she was very concerned for me and that it grieved her something bad that she had to let me go. Her husband told her, "You know we can't keep her."

As we left Chicago that morning, I felt like I was leaving a part of my heart behind. With all that was within me, I did not want to leave. For two weeks, no one had said a single cruel word to me. I had never imagined that anyone could be as kind as those people. From these short two weeks, I had come to the conclusion that all black people were naturally kind, that it was just in their nature to treat people with respect, even the thugs on the street. Before we were even out of the city, the kids on the bus were verbally attacking me again.

By the end of that summer, Pam introduced me to alcohol. One drink would not satisfy me. I had no control of my liquor. It controlled me. I would continue to drink until there was no more available, or I was sick to my stomach. Eventually I would pass out. My mother and her father's drinking problem had carried on to the next generation. I was an alcoholic at the age of fourteen. It was also through Pam that I started smoking.

She did not just get me into bad habits, though. She would prove to be a great help in building up my self-esteem. She told me one day to try holding my mouth slightly open, to see if it would help my facial features. With holding my jaw slightly open, I almost looked normal. It would be as simple as making this a habit. She taught me how to put on makeup. By the time Pam was done with me, aside from my curved spine, I looked pretty good.

I started high school that fall. Even though I was attending a special class intended for dummies, the class was still made up of two different classes of people—the upper class who thought they were high and mighty and the middle class. I did not fit into either category. I was in a rut that I could not break loose of, so once again I was made fun of and picked on by students who were no mightier than I. It seemed no matter what direction I turned, there would always be bullies.

The advice that Pam had given me had paid off, but the fear I had of my fellow students would still prove to hold me back. Within the first semester, the school decided to choose the prettiest girl from every class to run in a beauty contest. From these girls, the school would make their final choice for the Beauty Queen. After the girls of my class put some consideration into it, and they had eliminated one girl after another among themselves, they decided that I would run for Beauty Queen. They told me that as much as they did not like me, I was the prettiest one in the class. I did not trust them. I figured they were trying to set me up so they could make a fool out of me. I refused to do it, which only made them hate me more. You have to remember, all my life I grew up hearing that I was too ugly to be Peter Campbell's daughter. If a child hears only negative things, that is what they will grow up to believe.

Still, I had the two dreadful curves in my spine. Plus, from the side view, it was very easy to tell that there was something not right with my upper jaw. So still I would have been the laughingstock of the school. I had been through enough. The girls in my class were still blowing off steam when we got on the school bus later that day. I just stared out the side window believing if I paid no attention to their continual bickering, they would eventually shut up.

Suddenly, one of the boys spoke up. He said, "You don't believe you're pretty, do you?" This surprised me enough to glance up. He was the hottest looking boy on the bus. I had noticed him before, but of course I would never let on that I thought he was a hunk. I figured that he would be offended that a girl like me would find him cute. When I saw that it was Danny Rivets, and he was looking me straight in the eyes, I quickly lowered my face from his gaze. Again he spoke up: "You. You're the one I said was pretty." He then turned to another boy on the bus and said, "I bet you ten dollars Pattie will go out with me on a date."

That was when I was positive he had only said this to make fun of me. He then asked me to go out with him. I was afraid I would be laughed at. After that time babysitting, I was left very afraid of all boys and men. There was just no way I was going to go out with him, or any other boy. I was very timid. And so, in shyness, I shook my head no. But he would not stop chattering at me. "When you get home tonight," he said, "take a real good look in a full-length mirror. Look yourself over well, look at your legs, then look at your face, and see how attractive you are."

As soon as he mentioned my legs, he had my full attention. This was simply because he had not been the first to mention them. When I got home that night, I went right for the bedroom mirror and took a good, long look at myself. This was when I realized that I did not look as bad as I had thought. This was when I remembered the book called "The Ugly Duckling." I knew something good had finally happened to me. It felt nice when he spoke to me, but I had no idea what this feeling was. I never did run for the beauty contest, and it would be four more years before I would get up the nerve to start dating.

Our worst teacher was our homeroom teacher. She was a cold, cruel woman. She thought one day that she was alone with a Down Syndrome girl who attended her Grade Ten class. I was not supposed to be in there, but for some reason I had entered the classroom and saw the teacher making fun of the girl. She was laughing at the girl's disability. When I caught her, I gave her a dirty look. I told her she was disgraceful, useless, and ignorant, and that she was a poor excuse for a teacher. She told me that she would make my remaining time in her classroom miserable. It was bad enough that children had to be bullied by fellow students, but it was getting pathetic when teachers would act in such a shameful, uncalled-for manner.

Our best teacher was our math teacher. He had a good heart and treated his students with respect. From Grade One all the way up to Grade Ten, he turned out to be my favourite—and to be fully honest, I had a schoolgirl crush on him.

By the time I was in high school, I had pretty well given up to the point that I did not care whether I was in school or not. So it turned out that a great deal of my time was spent skipping classes. But I would seldom skip math. Although my learning disability made it impossible to learn anything, I believe math might have been my worst subject.

Not only was I a good artist, but I found it to be a refuge from life. I found that I could lose myself in my sketching, as though I was in another world. Through art, I could escape from all the pain and disappointments of the world. So when I was in math class, I would sit and sketch. It was like the teacher understood how much I needed this. He would actually mark my grades on my art. The grades he gave me were the best grades I ever received in all the years I attended school.

From my first day of Grade One to this day, school has given me nothing but grief. I lost count of how many nights I cried myself to sleep. Why? Because I had dreams. I was always a perfectionist. I expected everything I did and touched to turn into gold, but it seemed that as far as my education went, which was the most important achievement I would ever have to hurtle above, I had no hope of ever succeeding.

I had two weeks left until my sixteenth birthday. I would be walking out of school on March 22, to never return. I felt I did owe an explanation to the only teacher that had ever treated me with respect. I also wanted to say goodbye. And so I went to my math teacher and told him I was quitting school. He tried to talk me out of it. He told me that if I waited until the end of the semester, I would have my Grade Ten. But I had already made up my mind. It would not be changed.

On my last day of school, my math teacher gave me a slip of paper with an address on it. He told me to send some of my art sketches to that address and wait for their response. Immediately I sent some of my finest works of art. They wrote me back, asking for more sketches. This time they wanted me to be creative, by designing dresses on models. I sketched the dresses as they came to my mind and then sent this back. The next letter they sent almost blew my mind. Could it be true? Was there something I wasactually good at? They told me I was good, that they were actually offering to send me to Paris, France to be a designer.

I was looking at my letter with such excitement. I could scarcely believe what I had in my hands. Did this mean I could possibly become more successful than every one of the students I had attended school with? That was when Dad came in the room and took the letter out of my hand. After he read it, he said, "Do you really believe you're that good? You're not an artist. You can't draw. Your art is garbage. They are only trying to bring young girls over so they can use them for sex." He ripped up my letter, then he tossed it in the fire.

Dad had said a lot of painful things to me over the years, but this was the worst. My art was the only thing I could do well. He not only broke my heart with his cruel, thoughtless words, but also took the letter from me, which was the only hope I had ever received. Many years later, I was watching an awards show on TV when I saw Madonna come on stage. She was wearing one of the dresses I had sketched. Another time, I was watching the models on the catwalk, when I saw the other dress I had sketched. I know that I can never take the credit for these dresses, but believe me, that was incredible to see.

On my eighteenth birthday, Dad started taking me to the hotel with him and Mom. His excuse for this was that Mom drank so heavily that it made him feel lonely for someone to sit and talk with. He would not allow me to have alcoholic beverages. I know had he allowed me the alcohol, he would have had two drunks on his hands. The first night that I joined them in the bar, a man asked me up to dance. The whole night, right through to closing, he danced with me. I had fun and knew that

I was ready for dating. I had really hoped he would be back the next Saturday night, but that was not going to happen. Dad asked around about him and found out he was married.

As soon as my friend Bonny knew I was ready for boys, she set me up on a blind date. Earlier that day, we went to town to get some new clothes for our night out. She took me to the clothing store. Then she showed me a way to not get caught stealing clothing. Of course, we picked up clothes to wear that night. So that was what I wore on my blind date. Bonny took off with her date and left me alone with mine. My childhood hurts had still not healed, therefore I could scarcely talk. After sitting there for some time without hearing me say a word, he decided to break the boredom by raping me. He was too strong for me to fight off. He had me overpowered.

That was when I cried out, "Dear God, help me." It was only seconds after I cried out that Bonny and her date came back to the car. At this point, he had my pants and panties pulled down to my knees. When they came banging at the car window, he stopped and released me. I never even had time to think about why I was crying out to God. This would be one of the times God tried to get my attention. He rescued me, and yet I still did not believe in the Almighty God.

When I got home that night, I went directly to my dad and woke him. I said, "I have done a terrible thing. I went out with Bonny and stole clothing from a store in Goderich. I truly feel that I almost paid for what I did. I was nearly raped tonight." I told him I was not going to steal clothes again. After that, I never did steal clothes, but I did continue to steal. Like my dad, I had sticky fingers.

I was stubborn and I wanted to start dating. I thought that if I did not start going out with boys, I would become an old spinster. There was always someone rubbing my nose in to the fact that, compared to me, Cathy was well advanced. She was dating, and

I had not yet started. This was when I knew I had to learn how to outsmart the men.

It was my heart's desire to save my purity for my wedding night. My opinion was that if I had been more talkative on my date, he might not have tried to assault me. I also felt that not only was it important to give a good first impression, but I needed to dress sensibly, as to not entice my date to seduce me. Short skirts would not be suitable on a date, unless of course I was looking for trouble. I would also have to train myself to chatter continuously. The continual gabbing would distract my date enough that he would most likely not assault me.

The most marvellous article clothing I ever owned was my one-piece jumpsuit. It was very pretty. The colour was pail mint green. This garment was flattering to my appearance. Therefore, it gave a good first impression. Down the front of it were more than twenty teeny, awkward buttons. The button holes were just a tiny bit too small for the buttons, which made this praiseworthy jumpsuit nearly impossible to remove.

The continuous chatter came easy. I found the more I talked, the less nervous I was. Ninety-five percent of the time I spent with my date was consumed with me talking. During the time I was chattering, I would be dreaming up what to say next.

After I had gone out with several young men, Danny came to our home on a Saturday night. He wanted to double date with my sister and her friend. The movie "Love Story" had just been released, and it was playing at all the movie theaters. He wanted to take me to see this movie. That same warm, comfy feeling came back just as it had before whenever he was near. I had no plans of going out that night, but when he came to the door, I quickly changed my plans. I never dreamed being on a date could be that much fun. He had me laughing most of the night. I noticed he seemed to be enjoying the evening. I also noticed that he would not try to touch me in an inappropriate way.

It had been a long time since I had been treated so fine. I told him that I always got this strange feeling when he was near me. He only smiled and looked deep into my eyes. At that point, he looked proud. I swear if he had been a peacock, his beautiful tail would have been fully fanned out. After that evening, Danny and I went out steady for a couple of months. Every time we were together, it was like magic. Since I had never been raised to show such emotions, I had no idea what love was, or what it felt like. Therefore, I had no idea that this was love.

Cathy and I were in the habit of walking nine miles into town to meet our father at Dominion Roads, where he worked. When he got off at midnight, we would ride back home to the farm with Dad. This was something we would often do. One evening, we took off walking to Goderich with plans of heading home later with our father. Just as we were starting across the bridge into town, a car pulled over to offer us a ride. The driver was Fred, a young man Cathy had been just recently going out with. His friend Gerald was seated in the passenger seat. Since my sister knew the driver, we felt safe getting in and taking the ride. It was still quite early in the evening, so instead of heading right over to Dominion Roads, we went to a house party with the guys. As much as I did enjoy the evening, I had no interest in Gerald.

About a week later, Danny and I were out cruising with my dad's car. I was seated in the driver's seat. He had his arm around my shoulders, pressing his foot on the gas pedal while I steered. We were laughing, and romance was in the air. Suddenly a car was heading right for us. Gerald was driving the other car, and my dad was seated next to him. That was when Gerald spun his car around and cut Danny and I off. Dad came to the car and made me get into Gerald's car with him. I guess Dad must have taken Danny home. Gerald took me back to my home, where he waited until my dad got back.

As he was entering the house, my father told me that I was not to see Danny anymore. He said that he had gotten a bad report about him. Dad pushed the matter, insisting that I date Gerald. Not only that, but Gerald had told my father that he wanted to marry me. So now Dad was bent on the two of us getting married.

# CHAPTER 6

# MAKING THE RASH DECISION
# I WOULD REGRET

*D*ad reminded me that I did not have the intelligence to do anything more than babysit. He told me that I would need a man to care for me. Plus, Danny did not come back to the house after that day. So after two months of knowing Gerald, I married him.

Between Gerald and his sister Carry, I was forced to wear Carry's wedding gown. It was yellowed and torn. I protested against it, but nobody would side with me. I thought I did deserve a pretty white gown. Gerald came in the church late. He was so drunk that he could not even stand on his feet, so not only did I have to wear this hand-me-down dress, but he made a fool out of me by coming in drunk.

Early that evening, as we were heading off to Stratford, Ontario, Gerald forced me to ride in the backseat of the car. He told me that now that I was his wife, I was no more than dirt under his feet, and that from here on out, I would ride in the back. We would room and board until we had the first and last month's payment to put on an apartment. So our wedding night was spent in a boarding house. I was okay talking one on one with a person, but if there was more than one person in the room, I would clam up. I was very nervous, which made me uncomfortable. The lady of the house had our dinner ready for us when we came in. While we sat down to dinner, Gerald told the couple that he would be sexually active with whomever he wanted and have as many women on the side as he wished. He told them that I had no rights; I was only a woman.

That night as I laid in bed, I knew that I had made a big mistake. I had made a rash decision that I would regret. I had never heard of an annulment, so of course I had no idea what my rights were. Therefore, I felt there was no way out for me. Besides, maybe Dad was right about me not being able to take care of myself.

Stratford was like a city of factories. I had never dreamed there could be so many job opportunities in one place. We were married on a Saturday, and by late Monday morning, we were both hired and working. I worked at a factor that made filters. Gerald worked in a rubber factory. Although I did not believe in God, just the same I felt that a woman was responsible for providing her husband with pleasure, so although he was unfaithful to me, I never refused myself to him. The Apostle Paul put it this way:

> Nevertheless, because of sexual immorality, let each man have his own wife, and let each woman have her own husband. Let the husband render to his wife the affection due her, and likewise also the wife to her husband. The wife does not have authority over her own body, but the husband does. And likewise the husband does not have authority over his own body, but the wife does. Do not deprive one another except with consent for a time, that you may give yourselves to fasting and prayer; and come together again so that Satan

does not tempt you because of your lack of self-control. (1 Corinthians 7:2–5)

I wasted no time in getting my father a new woman friend. Cathy was moving out to get married. When Dad was not at home, Mom would be alone with Tammy and Sherry. I did not trust her alone with my younger sisters, so according to my logic the most sensible thing to do was to bring another woman into the picture. In less than six months, my father kicked my mother out. He then moved Cassie in. Cassie had five children of her own. I could see she was good with children. Therefore, everything went as planned.

Ninety percent of the time when Gerald was not at work, he was drunk. He would take all the money I would earn and put it towards his bad habit. I got enough money from my paycheque for a coffee, and that would be all I got for the next two weeks. He expected me to walk home every night from work. To get home, I had to pass by four hotels at closing time.

We were married five months when I became pregnant with my daughter. That spring, we moved back to Goderich, where we lived with his mother and father until I protested that I wanted our own home. All the time we were in his parents' home, Gerald and his sister were making sexual advances at each other. Whether I was in the room or not made no difference on how they would behave.

My husband was lazy. He would work six months, then quit his job and collect unemployment until it ran out. He would then get another job. He followed this cycle all through the time I was with him. He was most happy sitting in front of the TV with a beer. He tried a few times to set me up as a prostitute. He would make arrangements with a man, then bring him to our home where he would confront me with his decision. I am so glad my refusals ensured that none of this took place.

Shortly after we moved back to Goderich, Danny started to hang out with Gerald and me. The first opportunity he had alone with me, he told me that he had heard Gerald was abusing me. He had come back to protect me. What he may have been referring to was the night when Gerald punched me in the stomach and I went into false labour. As much as I loved Danny, still I remained faithful to my husband.

His adulterous acts were not a part of my imagination. More than once, I did see him in action. Gerald, Danny, and I were out cruising one afternoon when Gerald saw Darleen, a girl he knew, standing on a street corner. He pulled over to pick her up. She had it out for me. She was the promiscuous girl on the school bus. It was the same girl who had her nose out of joint when the boys whistled and howled at my legs. Gerald had not been her type until she saw that he was my husband. Then suddenly she was interested in him. She told him that she would only get in the car if I was forced to sit in the back seat, and she sat in the front with him. He was more than willing to shove me in the back. Danny right away went into the back with me.

Next, she offered to have sex with Gerald, but only under the condition that I would be forced to sit and watch. He was quick to head down a secluded dirt road and find a suitable place to park. I pleaded with my husband, but he had already made up his mind that I would be forced to watch. Danny grabbed me and rushed me into the bushes. He held me in his arms while I cried. At this time, Gerald committed adultery with Darleen. I stayed that night with my dad on the farm.

I was eight months pregnant and I felt as big as a house. I had tried for twelve months to make this marriage work, but everyone has a breaking point. When Gerald did this to me, it was the straw that broke the camel's back. I returned home to my dad.

The next day, my dad took me back into town and dropped me off. As I came into the house, Gerald told me, "Danny has been hanging around because he is in love with you. I told him to get out and not to come back. That is the last you will see of him." I found even being in the room with my husband repulsive. For the first time since our wedding day, I would not let him touch me. I took a heavy comforter and slept on the floor. For the next month, I slept there. I wanted to leave him, but I was still uncertain whether leaving was appropriate or not.

One month after the afternoon with Darleen, we were in our kitchen arguing when suddenly he took a knife that he carried in his boot. He carved my initials into our kitchen table. He told me, "Next time, I will use this knife on you." I knew then it was time to get out.

The night I left Gerald, I sat alone in the spare bedroom. It was past 11:00 at night, so there would be no one to check on me before noon the next day. I had often woke in the morning thinking about how it was only when I slept that all the pain and hurt would go away. But then when I woke up, again I had to face all the sadness. I was tired of living. Mom had told me there was no God, and therefore I'd come to the conclusion, that dying was like falling to sleep. And then it would never hurt again. Although Cathy had been moved out for a year, her sleeping pills were still in the medicine cabinet. The bottle was full, so there were enough pills to successfully commit suicide.

Quietly I made my way down the steps, into the bathroom. Just as I knew I would find them, the sleeping pills were in the cabinet, untouched. I took the pills. Then, entering the kitchen, I poured myself a glass of water. Back in the bedroom, I sat on the bed. All but for the faint light of the full moon, the room was dark. I opened the bottle of pills and emptied as many as I could hold into my hand. I raised my hand to my mouth, ready to take the pills, when suddenly my baby moved. That was when I realized that I was not taking one life; I was taking the life of my unborn child as well. I put the pills back in the bottle and slipped down the stairway. Then I put the bottle back just as I had found it.

As I lay in bed, I knew that after my baby was born it would need me. There was no way I would want either of my parents raising this child, not after what they'd done to me. Suicide was out of the picture. This child needed me. So that night I decided I would never again try to take my life.

Lying there, all my pain and hurt turned into anger. From the first time my father had spoken of the Italian prostitute right through Ricky's death. Every time someone made fun of my deformed jaw or my crooked back. Every time someone made fun of me because I could not talk. Or that I could not read or write. Or that I was ugly, mentally challenged, a circus sideshow freak.

Suddenly, it did not hurt. Instead I was angry beyond what most people can understand. Yes, I put the pills back. In order to look good to his mother, Gerald told her I was the one who had been unfaithful. Okay, I would be the bad girl. After this baby was weaned, I would do the very thing he had accused me of. I would be an adulteress woman. When I was done, he would hang his head in shame. Not only him, but that useless father of mine as well. I would get even with them for what they had done to me.

From our wedding day to the day I left him, I lived with Gerald fourteen months.

# CHAPTER 7

# MAKING IT ON MY OWN

*I* was in my tenth month when I finally went into labour. Cassie took me to the Goderich Hospital. My family doctor was on holidays, leaving me with no physician. At this point, my water broke. I would stay in this hospital for the next two weeks. My labour was strong, plus I was in a great deal of pain. The contractions would only go so far, but then they would stop and start again from the beginning. I would then go through the contractions as before. This would repeat itself continually for the next two weeks. Because the doctor had left no orders for my care, legally no one could touch me, nor could any doctor or nurse make a decision as to what should be done next. Therefore, I was left in hard labour for two weeks. My dad and Cassie took me out of the hospital. I rode on a cot in the back of my father's van.

They took me to the Old Victoria Hospital in London. Entering the hospital, I was taken right to the maternity ward. Without delay, they were doing an ultrasound on my baby. Her heart was failing. It was also discovered that the baby's head was tilted back and forced against my cervix. There was a blockage preventing her from passing through the cervix. I believe it would have been the lower curve in my spine that prevented the baby from passing through, which prevented her from going through the birth canal. The doctor told Dad and Cassie that if they wanted this baby to live, they had better get down on their knees and start praying. The only thing that was going to save it was a miracle.

Immediately I was taken into surgery for a Caesarean section. The surgery was so rushed that I was not quite out when they started to cut in. I can remember the cold knife blade on my skin. It would be twelve days before I would see my baby. Up to then, they would keep putting me back under. Therefore, I have very little memory of the two weeks I stayed in hospital. When I was put out for surgery, the last words I heard were, "The baby's heart has stopped. It's dying."

I woke up in a small, dark room. I could see the clock on the wall from where I lay. Every time I woke up, there was a nurse in my room who would give me a needle without delay. And I would be out again. The third time this happened, I asked if my baby was alive. She got a horrified look on her face and quickly rushed to once again put me to sleep.

This time my heart failed. They were now fighting to keep me alive. The next time I woke up, my dad and Cassie were in the room. They were smiling at me. A nurse came around the corner of the bed and showed me a paper with a tiny footprint and something else on it. She told me I had a baby girl. Cassie told me that Dad and her had been praying for me and my baby. The only other time I could remember my father praying was when I was a small child, when he taught me my bedtime prayer.

They also told me the baby was across the street in the Sick Children's Hospital. I later found out that she was kept there for twelve days while they fought to keep her alive. My baby's heart would keep stopping. The first time I remember holding her was when I sat in the wheelchair, ready to go home. The nurse put my bundled baby in my arms and Dad and I headed back home to the farm.

While traveling home, he asked me if I had chosen a name for my baby. I knew that Gerald had chosen a name—Samantha May—but that was not the name I had intended to give her. Out of respect for him, I did give her the name he chose. As much as I was still groggy from my stay in the hospital, I knew she was just too sweet to be a Samantha May, and so as much as she did receive the name her father chose, I nicknamed her Candy, after a young girl who had shown extreme kindness to me for a period of time during my painful childhood.

On our way home, Dad stopped at a trailer park and helped me to purchase a house trailer so that Candy and I would have a home. It would take over a month before all the legal paperwork would be finished. Therefore, I spent the first two months in the house with Dad and Cassie. Since I found the first few months as a new mother difficult, living in the farmhouse with them was a blessing. My father had my home parked in the field next to the farmhouse. That way, should I need their help, they were close by. Within a week of coming home with my new baby, I was set up for welfare. Within days, I was also on Mother's Allowances, receiving a monthly income. As soon as I was strong enough, I got myself a job as a dishwasher in a nearby inn. This was mainly to prove that I could make it on my own.

Although I was only a dishwasher, just the same I was bringing home good pay. Marrying Gerald had changed my last name from Campbell to Lee. I would sign my name as Pat Lee. My paycheques were more than enough to cover all my expenses. But sadly enough, all good things must come to an end.

Candy was a beautiful child, but at the age of two we discovered that she was having some difficulties. She was not yet talking and her motor skills were not developing. That was when she and I went back to the Sick Children's Hospital in London. I found out that the heart difficulties at birth had caused irreversible brain damage. Therefore, I had to quit my job and go back on to Mother's Allowance so that I could spend more time helping her develop her motor skills. And also, to teach her to talk. While we stayed in London, I was trained on how to go about this, using the learning skills they had taught me.

Candy was only a few months old when I laid down on my side on a stack of books. My intention was to try to straighten my spine. I wanted to improve my appearance. Although I did improve it well enough to be barely noticeable, what I did succeed in doing was adding two more curves to my spine. After this, I started bringing in men to be sexually involved with. I didn't even know the first names of ninety percent of the men I slept with. My main intention was to hurt the people who had hurt me. I have no count of how many men there was.

Early in my promiscuous lifestyle, I became pregnant. I was terrified. Not only did I not have any clue who the father was, but my bad experience with giving birth had left me paranoid with fear. I did the unthinkable. Abortions were illegal, and for that reason I performed my own. This did not help me to learn my lesson, however. I continued in my bad lifestyle.

When I look back at those days, I am astonished how God protected me. I did not deserve His love or protection. I was not divorced from Gerald, and even if I had been, fornication is still a sin. The only sex that is proper in God's eyes is that which takes place between a husband and his wife. No matter how you look at what I did, it was sin. I committed adultery in the eyes of God.

One night, I woke to see my oil furnace white-hot. I knew an angel had woken me. There was no smoke, smell, or excessive heat to warn me. Without the divine power of God, I would have never woken up. The other amazing thing was that I was still married to Gerald. I did not know even the first name of the man who lay in bed next to me. I had a memory elapse from the time I set my eyes on the oil furnace to after the danger was over and it had cooled off. The man who shared my bed told me he was terrified, and he was totally amazed at how calmly and swiftly I moved.

I know it was the Spirit of God. I also know I did not deserve what He did for me. Me, my baby, and that man within moments would have died if I had not woken when I did. I believe the furnace was ready to blow. I read that white-hot steel runs like water. God is great. He is almighty.

One afternoon, I heard a knock at my door. When I came to answer the door, it was Danny. Suddenly I felt disgraceful. I felt dirty. I was ashamed of what I had become. I quickly let him in. It was such an awkward feeling. As he stood in front of me, I found myself regretting everything I had done. Instead of that warm, happy feeling I always got when he came in the room, I was feeling shame. I was so full of fear that while he was there with me, a man would come to the door expecting shameful acts from me. In my simple way of thinking, I felt I had slept with all those men and that it meant nothing. But Danny was different. I took him and led him into my bedroom and made love to him. I had no idea what it felt like to be with someone you loved.

It was only afterwards when he was watching nervously out the front window that I spoke up. "Danny, please take me and Candy away from here. I have made a serious mistake. I want to be with you. I want to leave this place."

He turned to me and said, "Take Candy over to your dad's. Ask him if he would watch her for a half-hour, but don't tell him it's me you're going out with."

After I got back, Danny took me out in the car he had showed up with. He told me that he was in trouble with the law. He said he had done a very bad thing and that he would never come back out of jail alive. He told me that he was going to die in there. I told him about the warm feeling I got every time he drew near me, and that I didn't understand what it was. He brushed my cheek with his hand and said, "They call it love, Pattie. You fell in love with me the day I told you to look in the mirror. That was also the day I fell in love with you."

In silence, I stared into his face. I spoke up and said, "All these years I have wasted. And you were the one."

I heard a siren as Danny put the gas pedal to the floor. When I looked behind us, I saw a police cruiser. We were in a high speed chase. After he lost the police cruiser, he took me home and told me, "I came back to say goodbye. I just wanted to say I love you. I will never forget you, nor will I forget that magic moment we spent back at your home. I have never been so afraid as I was today, when I thought something could have happened to you. I want you to promise me that you will stop taking these men into your home. Please promise me that you will get married and make a good home for your little girl." I pleaded with him, saying that I only wanted him.

"Don't wait for me," he said. "I will never come out of there alive. You are the only one I have ever loved."

I watched as he drove away. Somewhere deep inside, I hoped he was wrong. He never came back. He was my first love. You never stop loving your first.

I decided that day that I would not live this promiscuous lifestyle any longer. I found out that this was not going to be as easy as just saying it, though. The men were coming to my home and hounding me. When I tried to make them leave, they would not go. I knew I had myself in a fine mess. That was when I packed up my mobile home and headed for a small town called Mount Forest.

By the time I had moved to Mount Forest, Dad and Cassie had been living there for a few months. Dad had a pasture that he ran his horses in. This was where my trailer was set up. This was the most primitive I had ever lived. There was no running water, no electricity, and had it not been for my gas stove hook-up, there would have been nothing to cook on. I lived like that right through the summer into the early fall. I collected our drinking water from the creek that ran through the horse's pasture land. My toilet was a five-gallon pail.

It was here that I met Bob. I was much more careful now to not give the men the idea that I was a tramp. I thought I was a lady when I made Bob wait one month before we were intimately involved.

After dating him for a couple of months, I was out cruising with him when suddenly I got the most painful stomach ache. Immediately he took me to the hospital. The doctor on-call told us that my uterus had been badly damaged. He told me that every time I would get pregnant, my uterus would abort the baby. He put me on the birth control pill to prevent this from happening. I had never taken any form of birth control, as no one had ever spoken to me about it.

It was shortly after this that it got too cold to live in the trailer home. I moved in with Cassie and Dad for the winter. By this time, she and Dad had a son together. She was great with small children, and to this day my younger sisters love her greatly. She was perfect for them. However, I was not close to her, and living there was not my idea of peace and joy.

That night, I had an experience I would never forget. I slept on a sofa in the small family room on the main floor. As I lay on my back, my thoughts ran wild. I remembered my father's cruel words when I was growing up, how my brother died, how everyone had hurt me—Gerald, teachers, students, and so many others. My thoughts also went to the black lady in Chicago who had cared for me. I missed Danny and knew he would never come back. I remembered all the evil things I had done. I was lonely and afraid. If ever I needed God, it was now.

I remembered the nice feeling I'd had in the church in Chicago. It was at this point that I looked up and cried out, "You, God, who the Jehovah Witnesses say is real, prove yourself to me now, or I will never call to you again."

As I spoke that last word, I felt my soul divide from my body. It was my spirit starting to rise up. The street light caused a faint glow in the room. As my soul rose from the room, the faint light disappeared. I was surrounded by darkness. As I rose higher, a white circle started to appear. As my spirit came closer to the circle, I saw that it was revolving in a clockwise direction. The closer I got to it, the more apparent it became that the circle was made up of heavenly beings. My soul entered into the midst of the heavenly angels. As they revolved around me, they brushed me with their wings. I had no idea how to address the Almighty God with respect and reverence. I did not know how to pray. What I said next just came out of me as an impulse. I started to cry out, "My God, you're real, you're real…" I started to laugh. I was chanting over and over again. "You're real, you're real," when suddenly I felt fatigue. Then I said, "I'm tired. I want to go back." At that very moment, I fell asleep.

I woke the next morning on the sofa as though nothing had happened the night before. But I knew there was a God. I believed. I rushed up to Dad and Cassie's room. Knocking at the door, I did not even give them a chance to invite me in. I opened the door and rushed in, shouting, "He is real! God is real! Mom told me there was no God, but no, He is real!" I explained to Dad my experience from the night before. He told me it had to be just a dream, but I said, "No, Dad. I was in the midst of angels. It was not a dream."

Close to two months had passed when I started getting sick to my stomach. This would happen every day. I started forming a round belly, and I had gained an appetite. It was then that I became aware that I was expecting a baby. My reaction to this was fear. My delivery of Candy was enough to give me nightmares. I stood in the basement of my dad's house, rubbing my hands together as I trembled with fear. I did not like the mother I had become. It did not seem right to bring another child into my care.

The abuse I experienced as a child still haunted me as an adult. As much as I said I would never be like my parents, I believe I had turned out worse. I know today how deep my love for my children was then, and how deep my love is for them now, but before I actually accepted Jesus into my heart I had no way of feeling experiencing love. It was almost like my heart was inactive. I could not feel emotional compassion or love. Something in my soul had been destroyed. I loved Candy. God had to know how much I loved her, but something was not right with me. I did unforgivable things to my child. One time while she was just toddling, and she had only started taking a few steps on her own, I was in a hurry and kicked my little girl when she got in the way. She went tumbling to the floor. I was horrified that I could do such a terrible thing to my baby. I did not even pick my child up. I could not be the mommy I wanted to be.

I knew something was not right with me. I told myself, "I will never do that again." But that was never the case, because next time I would do it again. I had the greatest fear that my little girl would later remember how bad a mommy I had been. I wanted her to know that I loved her. I never intended to hurt my child. I found myself avoiding cuddling her. The only reason why I did it was because Cassie would not let up about it. Later I got so I would actually enjoy it. I told her everyday that I loved her, but I was so afraid that my actions spoke different.

Bob was very attached to his mother, May. Up to this point, Bob and his mother had not been pleased with the fact that I was expecting. May was a highly respected woman in the village. She never missed a Sunday morning church service. And even to me, bringing another child into this life seemed like a sin.

An angel appeared then and told me, "Don't be afraid. Don't harm the child. Everything will be okay." As the angel was leaving, the phone rang. Bob told me, "I am on my way over. Mom is okay with everything. She wants you and Candy to live here with us." By the next spring, May had my trailer home on their family farm. I had a well, electricity, and all the essentials needed for survival. After I became a Christian, I knew God healed my uterus. He did not want me in the field drinking water from a creek. I wanted to draw close to God. I started attending church with Bob's mother. She attended the Anglican Church. I also discovered I could read the Bible without difficulty.

While I was still expecting, May bought me a large hardcover children's storybook. In it was every story from the Bible. It had large full colour pictures that children could really enjoy. I started reading it to Candy right away. It seemed that after my out-of-body experience, I got more comfortable with cuddling her. So this turned out to be a special time for both of us. Again, to my amazement, I found that it was easy to read this book. But I found anything that was not in connection with the Bible practically impossible to read.

My second child was a boy. I named this child James Richard, after my baby brother who had died. I called him Jamie, for short. His birth went much better. I had an excellent doctor who watched my pregnancy and delivery carefully. He set a date for a Caesarean section. My baby was safely delivered. I got the feeling that this doctor may have been a Christian.

I would like to tell you that I was a good mother after my encounter with God, but that was far from the truth. At least I can say that I did improve. I did much better with Jamie as an infant than I had with Candy. I made bedtime very special, to the point that they would look forward to their bedtime. On the outside, we looked like a healthy, functional family. Outsiders would exclaim how well I did at raising two small children on my own. I knew Candy and Jamie were little gems, but behind closed doors I was abusive. My children got punished quite often when they should have never been. I did not like my temper. I was fearful to touch my children. Regardless which child it is, all children tend to test one's patience.

My painful past left me with a bad temper. It would take very little to cause me to blow. When they tested me to this point, I would make them go to their room until I felt safe that I would not hurt them in such a way that I would regret. But sometimes that did not work. I regret the times when I overreacted. I wish

I could take that back. The thing that I feared the most was the strong urge I had to sexually assault my children. I had always considered the innocence of a child to be as precious as the tenderness of a drop of dew on a rose pedal. After my out-of-body experience, I saw children as a tender gift from God, and yet seeing my children naked gave me the most unbearable desire to touch them in ways that made me sick. This bad urge would start to haunt me when my child was as young as two years of age. It was so strong that I could not even be in the same room with my children to bathe them. Therefore, I had to stand outside the bath room while my six-year-old and two-year-old bathed themselves.

My fear that my small children could slip and drown in the tub, however, was overwhelming. I wanted someone to help me. I wanted to tell someone about my problem, but I was so terrified of Children's Aid. I thought that if I told anyone my problem, they would come in and take my babies away. My children were my angels. They were all I had.

Candy was thirteen when one day she started to undress while I stood in her bedroom with her. I raised my voice at her, shouting, "Don't you ever take your clothes off in my presence." She did not understand. I believe I might have frightened her. She thought because we were both women, there was nothing immoral with her undressing in front of her mother. The problem was not with my daughter; it was me. I know today that she never understood how much I loved her then, nor does she understand today how important she is to me. With great joy I can say that I never touched my children, nor any other child, in a sexually offensive way.

Jamie was under two years old when Bob and I ended our friendship. We ended on good terms. He was one of the best friends I ever had. I moved back with my dad. He was now separated from Cassie. They were in a battle over my little brother Jim, who was his child through Cassie. He had moved back to Goderich. It was not a good idea for me to follow him there, but

I truly had no other place to go, so I lived with my father until I was financially secure enough to be back on my own with my children.

To my dismay, as much as I truly enjoyed the town of Goderich, as soon as I returned I once again had men hounding me. I would not even go near any men while I was living there. I was terrified to trust anyone. By the time I had come back, Gerald and I were divorced. I found a pleasant church where I was warmly welcomed. The pastor of the Baptist Church came to my father's home and led me in asking Jesus into my heart. Instantly I felt a spiritual change. But the Devil was not willing to let me go.

Cathy asked me to come over to her home. She told me there were spiritual problems going on, and that she was afraid. She told me that her problems resembled closely the spiritual activities that had been happening on the farm when we were young. Her husband Fred had picked up a kit to build a gas motor. He had his finished motor sitting full of gas on top of the refrigerator. Next to the refrigerator was the gas cook stove. No one had switched the stove on, nor had anyone lit the pilot light, and yet Cathy could smell gas. She went into the kitchen and saw the gas motor lift off the refrigerator and drop down on the lit stove burner. I was afraid for her and her family. I wasted no time getting to her home.

My sister and her husband had had our mother living with them for a number of years. When I got there, I saw that my mother was playing with the Ouija board I had given her only a few years before. Immediately I saw the evil that was associated with this board. I felt bad that it had been a Christmas gift from me, but just the same I knew it had to go. I told her, "Mom, that board is evil. You are talking to bad spirits. It has to go."

No one had spoken to me about good and bad spirits. The only experience I had with spirits was while I was growing up, with the influence I received from my mother. Of course, this knowledge came from the Holy Ghost. I told her what Cathy had told me, of what was going on in the house. I also told her that such happenings could easily cause a house fire. I told her that this was the same things that had been happening when we were children, and that calling on the dead caused the trouble.

When she heard this, my mother was full of fear. She told me that she wanted the board out of the house. I wasted no time in calling the pastor of the church I attended. When I explained to him what was going on, he told me not to do anything to the board. He told me it had to be burned, but that it was too dangerous for me to do. What he wanted me to do was take the board from my mother and give it to him. He came to my sister's home and met me at the door. I took the board out of my mother's hands and took it to the door, then placed it in the pastor's hands. After he left, I asked my mother if she wanted to have Jesus as her personal Saviour. That night, she asked Jesus to be her Lord. Mom's life totally changed. She stopped drinking, she no longer did fortune-telling, she quit smoking, and she started attending church on a regular basis.

At some time, a spirit guide had entered me. I believe this might have been the time when it took place. That night, I started hearing voices in my head. I did not like it. Something did not feel right. I went back to the pastor and told him what was going on. He got all excited and told me, "That is God. He does not talk to just anyone. You are blessed. Answer him when he talks to you. Do whatever he tells you to do."

I had been taking my Bible and reading a chapter per day. The voice told me to change my way of reading it. From then on, I was to take it and let it drop open. Where ever my eyes fell, I was to read that section only. It did not take long before I realized I did not like what it had me reading. I would be told to not read the full paragraph. I would land on ones like Isaiah 20:3—"Walk naked and barefoot in the street" (paraphrased). One that I often opened to was Deuteronomy 13:9—"You shall surely kill him."

Of course I did not do the things asked of me. But when I decided I did not want to read my Bible this way anymore, the voice threatened me. Out of fear, I was therefore submissive to the way it chose that I read my Bible. I knew no better than this. I honestly believed it was God.

It was during the time that I attended this church that Candy received a healing of her own learning disability. Overnight, she went from failing every class to being a straight-A student. After that, school was a breeze for her. The girl never had to study to get these grades.

My Dad was grieved that I would not date any men throughout the time I was living with him in Goderich. It was an insult that his daughter did not have a man friend. He tried to talk me into going to the singles dance with him. I had heard nothing but bad things about it, so I refused to go. However, he would not let up. I knew he would not set foot in a church, so I gave him an ultimatum—"If you go to church with me, I will go to the singles dance with you." To my surprise, the following Sunday he went to church with me. In return, the following Saturday night I went to the dance with him.

It was natural that I would miss the companionship of a gentleman friend. Therefore, when a young man from across the room came up to me and asked to dance, as much as I was afraid to trust anyone, I did get up to dance with him. When he told me that he lived in London, Ontario, I felt safe that he was most likely not interested in me because of my bad reputation. In the short span of one song, I learned that he was Catholic. He was a middle child from a family of twelve children, of which eleven were living. One had died in a hit-and-run accident. Plus, he was French. He introduced himself as Maurice Loranger and asked if he could come courting the following Friday.

I had a comfortable feeling with him, so I agreed to this. After that one dance, he left. Right away, Dad then asked me to dance. In total excitement, he said, "Tell me all about him."

I told him what I knew he would not like. "He's French, and he's Catholic. He asked if he could come courting next Friday, and I said yes."

My father snorted and said, "You always pick the losers."

The following Friday night, I waited for nearly two hours. My dad came in the room and asked me where my date was. I smiled and said, "It looks like I got stood up." Ten minutes later, Maurice came to the door and apologized for being late. I would continue to date Maurice, and then marry him three years later.

I had a stalker who became a serious problem to me after Maurice came into my life. He would sexually assault me on the street, in broad daylight. Every time I would try to step out the door, without fail he would show up. He had no morals. He was making my life miserable. I was so fearful that he could try forcing his way into my home that I installed four locks on both of my outside doors.

One afternoon, he again came after me and started to assault me as before. That was when a woman came running up to us. She leaped on him, knocking him down to the pavement. She was a large girl and strong for a woman. She sat down on top of him. He could not get out from under her. His face turned beet red. I thought it looked good on him. She put one hand out to shake my hand and said, "Hi, I'm Evelyn. We met years ago. Looks like you need a bodyguard. Would you like to hang out?" I gladly took her on as a friend. Rain or shine, she was at my apartment every day. I did not go out without her. If she was with me, he would not touch me. She turned out to be a very loyal friend.

Maurice would go out to the local restaurant for coffee with the guys every weekend. They thought they were doing him a favour by telling him they saw this man harassing me. Because I had been a bad girl, they just assumed that was what I was doing. That's when I told Maurice the truth about my past. It went okay for I while, but then he said he just simply could not take any more of this. He was splitting up with me. I pleaded with him to take me out of this town. I knew living here was not going to get any better, so he helped me find an affordable apartment in Ingersoll, only nine miles outside of London.

It was at the time that I moved into my apartment that Dad got himself a new girlfriend. On first acquaintance, I came off strong enough that I know I scared her. I always had a bad experience with the women my father chose, so when Debby came along I expected no different. I was a grown woman now, and no one was going to walk all over me. At first sight of her, I said, "Cross me, and I'll nail you to the wall." She looked so afraid, I thought she was going to break out in tears. That was when I went silent. Somehow I knew in my heart that she had been abused as a child, possibly even as badly as I had been. Someone hurting another person was quite simply something I would not tolerate, so after that first acquaintance I softened towards her.

I was visiting with her one afternoon when suddenly she started to move towards my son like she intended to burn his skin with her lit cigarette. I spoke up quickly, saying, "Debby, what are you doing?" She snapped to attention and stopped in her tracks. Looking at her face, I knew she was not aware of what she had almost done. It looked to me like she was in a trance. I knew now without a doubt that someone had badly hurt her.

Living right next door to my sister's home made it pretty well impossible to not notice the people coming in and going out of her front door. One day, I saw a man going into her home. He was with a younger woman that I assumed was his wife. Something inside of me told me he was Debby's father. I boldly marched over to my sister's home. I told him, "I know who you are. You're Debby Teabolt's father. Only a snivelling coward would hurt a child as you did to Debby."

"Everything she told you was a lie," he said.

I told him, "She never told me anything about you."

Years later, I did get her to share a little from her childhood. The tiny bit she did share was shocking. She only gave me a couple of small details of the abuse she had suffered. Then she told me that she did not want to talk about it any further. I knew from the little she told me that the abuse she went through was outrageous. I was right about her Dad.

Debby ended up marrying my dad. She gave him a daughter, named Rebecca. Debby and I became best friends. Although the miles keep us apart, she is still dear to my heart.

Along with the help of a friend, Maurice moved me from the town of Goderich to Ingersoll, about a seventy-five miles away. I moved on my daughter's birthday, December 1. I then started to attend the Catholic church with Maurice. I had attended several denominations while seeking the church that I felt I fitted into best.

It was then that all spiritual chaos broke out. I was in the privacy of my bedroom one day, changing my clothes, when I saw a shadow move towards me. It frightened me, so I jumped up and ran out of the room. When I came back in, I could feel the presence of something lingering in there. Later through the night, in a dream I saw a man coming from behind me. He walked in front of me and stood at the foot of my bed, facing me. He then climbed on top of me. I woke up as I was being raped. I was terrified to go back to sleep. This would happen every night. When Maurice came to visit, I told him what was happening to me. To my relief, he believed me. I remembered that in the horror movies I had watched with my mother, they hung garlic to ward off vampires, so in my own simple way of thinking I asked Maurice to ask his mother for a crucifix to hang over my bed.

This did not help, and the problem got worse. Whether spirits can do this or not, I don't know, but he would take my soul up above my body while I slept so that I could look down at myself. Then, at a massive speed, he would send my soul spinning like a toy top. I was terrified. I wanted to wake up, but I could not. Only when I pleaded with God to help me would I awaken. I was terrorized every night by this evil spirit.

I had remained on Mother's Allowance ever since I was told to stay home with my child, since she needed extra special care. It had been my heart's desire to give my children a white-framed home with a large fenced-in yard. I found in Ingersoll the little house I had dreamed about all those years before. I knew that all the other stay-at-home moms who collected Mother's Allowance checks lived in low income housing, but I did not want my children growing up in that environment. Because of the drug and alcohol abuse in the area, I did not find these low income homes suitable to raise my children in. Most of the time I would not touch alcohol, because I knew I could not control it. I did not want my children to see me intoxicated. I didn't want anyone else drinking in the presence of my children, either.

I could also see from my kitchen window the school that Candy attended. I had a full view of the schoolyard where she played. Also, that fall Jamie would be starting kindergarten. It was comforting for me to know that I could still watch over my children, even while they were at school. In many ways, this little white house was perfect.

I have no idea what set them off, but one day Mother's Allowance decided they were going to cut me back by a large enough percentage that it would make providing for my children impossible. This happened in January. The landlord had just recently increased my rent by ten dollars. By the time I covered my bills and paid my rent, there was scarcely enough money left to buy food. Therefore, I stopped eating. Only my children ate. My refrigerator was empty, and I was too proud to ask for help. This was not the first time I had done this. There was one other time when I had stopped eating to provide for my children. That time, I did not eat for close to three months.

Out of desperation, I decided in the later part of January to ask Maurice to marry me. To my relief, he accepted my proposal. We were married on March 21, one day before my birthday. He was financial very stable. Therefore, I knew my children would have a roof over their heads and food on the table. Almost immediately after that, Maurice and I started verbally and physically abusing each other. It was not his fault; we were both products of highly dysfunctional homes.

In our third year of marriage, a married man started becoming very friendly towards me. I was miserable enough at home that this made it hard to resist his continual flirtations. He was a charmer, and he knew how to use all the right words to lure his victims in. I needed affection and he was offering it to me. Therefore, I fell into temptation and committed adultery. I had no clue what love felt like. I had mistaken lust for love. Although I felt guilty for my actions, this selfish and conniving affair lasted six months.

His wife was a gentle person. She had muscular dystrophy, which I was fully aware of. If that was not enough, she trusted me and thought I was her friend. I had to carry the guilt of that on my shoulders. Without making me aware of his intentions, he told her that he was leaving her for me. Then he took it upon himself to tell Maurice. In the end, my children, his children, his wife, and my husband were all badly hurt—not to mention all the close relatives on both sides of our families.

Debby had believed in me and was shocked at what I'd done. After my sin was revealed, the guilt of it was just too heavy a burden to carry. I felt I had to get to a minister and redo my sinner's prayer. It was a Baptist pastor who had prayed with me the first time, so of course it was a Baptist pastor I went to.

This time, I had given my husband a good reason to smack me around. Although it was in a subtle way, his violence worsened over time. Out of shame and fear, while Maurice was at work I took my kids and headed to a women's shelter. I was terrified of my husband and therefore had no intention of returning. While in there, I had to make a decision. If I left him, he would lose the house. That was not fair, since I was the one who had sinned.

He would be forced to pay child support for my children, which was also not fair, as he was not the man who had fathered them.

With all the cruelty we were undergoing, my kids still loved him. They were missing their dad. So again I went to church. This time it was the Salvation Army. The officer I spoke to had Maurice and I come in to see him as a couple. Maurice promised he would not hurt me if I came home, and so I went back home that day. The following Sunday, we went to the Salvation Army church, but I found that the people who attended the church acted as though I was an adulterous woman who should be stoned. Maurice and I did not go back.

A girlfriend who had for some time been trying to get me to accept Jesus as my Lord decided to take me to a deliverance service. She told me that I had an adulterous spirit in me, and that I needed it removed. I was horrified that I could do this again. I was more than willing to go and be set free of this horrid thing. At this service, they called all those who had bad spirits in them up to the front of the room. I hurried to get up there. When the prophets laid their hands on these people, they would go down in the spirit. But I was the only one left standing.

After the service was over and we were gathering our coats, the man who had prayed over me came to speak with me. He told me that the spirit within me was strong. This concerned me, because I wanted the spirit out so badly. He asked me if I wanted the gift of the Holy Spirit. I thought I would do anything just to get this spirit out of me, so I nodded my head yes and allowed him to guide me back up to the front. He told me to just let my tongue rest and not try to talk. He started speaking in the foreign language I had heard in the small church in Chicago. Shortly after this, my tongue started to move on its own. This language was coming from my mouth as well.

From there, I went to the Catholic Church and confessed my sins. The priest got very angry at me. He would not forgive me of my sins. From what I had been taught in this church, I understood that the priest had to forgive me before God could. This frightened me, because I knew I had sinned and needed God's forgiveness. I had remembered my sister-in-law once telling me that the Pentecostal Church was an excellent church. So that was my next choice.

# CHAPTER 8

# MY LORD, MY GOD

*I* entered Hi-Way Pentecostal Church for a Wednesday night Bible study. I did not want anyone to notice me. I was hoping to come in and go out without speaking to anyone. The first thing I noticed was that I got that same comfortable feeling here as I had gotten in the church in Chicago. When the study was over, I quickly got up from my chair, but before I could get to the door, the pastor caught me. I felt comfortable with him. I also felt like I had to confess my sin in order to be forgiven, so I told him about my affair and how badly I had hurt this woman who had trusted me. To my surprise, he did not treat me like a Jezebel but instead showed kindness. This left me at peace. Now I could feel certain that I had been forgiven.

After that night, I would continue to attend this church. I slowly made one friend after another. I found the people to be kind and warm-hearted. One Sunday morning, we had a visiting pastor speak to us named Pastor Morden. He was freshly out of Bible college and a little nervous. As he was finishing his sermon, the Lord spoke to him that there was a certain person in the congregation who was full of anger and hatred. He tried to call the person to the altar. I knew it was me, but there was no way I was going up there. I waited until everyone had left the sanctuary, then went up. He was still at the altar when I made my way up. I told him that I was the person full of anger and hatred. God started His healing process on me that day. I have heard it said, "He is working on the inside, changing me on the outside." That is just what He was doing with me.

Our pastor decided that he wanted to come to our home to visit Maurice. My husband asked Jesus to come into his heart. At this time, I wondered if I had said this prayer with true repentance or not. So again I received Jesus, when Maurice did. All counted, I repented and invited Jesus to be my Lord three times.

The abuse I received as a child haunted me as an adult. I could not feel tender love, nor could I give or receive it. It was like there was an empty cavity in my heart. It was almost like my heart was inactive. I could not feel emotional compassion or love. I had a husband and children, but I had no feeling towards them. One time, I stood between a Doberman Pincher and my son, to protect him from being attacked, but I felt nothing. Until I was thirty-three years old, my heart was dormant. Then I asked Jesus to come into my heart.

The pastor at our church would often speak on love. I had no idea what love was. I had only heard this word used when a man would say "I love you" to state the fact that he wanted to have sex. Therefore, I only understood it to be a four-letter word for sex. I had read 1 Corinthians 13:13—*"And now abide faith, hope, love, these three; but the greatest of these is love."* I wanted to feel this for my husband and children. I wanted to give them love. In the privacy of my home, I knelt down and asked God to teach me to love. When you ask God for something that serious, He is quick to give. He answered my prayer spontaneously.

I have no idea what conditional love feels like. I have never loved that way. God gave me agape love, His way of loving. Back in those days, Maurice was not easy to live with. Last Christmas, my daughter disowned me. Over the years, many people did hurtful things to me and to those who are dearest to me. I love my husband and children. I feel love for all of God's creation. There is no one I don't feel compassion for. I heard on the evening news one day about the mother and grandmother who came into a room and found their tiny infant torn to death by a dog. I had no idea who those people were, but I cried for days after I heard this. My heart was breaking for the family that lost their baby. I did not know them, but I loved them.

The love I can now feel is the love that God has for us. Nothing we can say or do can make Him love us any less, and so it is with me—unconditional love.

The cruel act I did to that family, and to mine, would eat at me like cancer. I regretted that I had committed adultery and wished that I could go back and make everything right. But there was no correcting this. Therefore, I spent most of my time drowning my sorrow in a bottle of wine. I would often skip Sunday morning service and instead go to the restaurant were my girlfriend worked. There I would drink until I had no more cash in my pocket. That was the way I lived for the first six years that I attended Hi-Way Pentecostal Church.

It was on the night of our tenth wedding anniversary when things changed. I was drunk to the point that I could not stand up. That was when the Holy Spirit spoke, "You can't serve both me and the bottle. You're going to half to choose between me and the alcohol. What if the parents of the children you teach Sunday school to saw you like this? They would no longer want you to teach their children. You can't serve the Devil and me at the same time." That was the blow that caught my attention. I never drank again after that night.

It was at the time I started going to Hi-Way Church when Candy started getting into a bad crowd. We tried everything we could think of to straighten her out, but nothing was working. We told her that she had to straighten out and respect the rules in our home, or she would have to get out. She was only fourteen, so that was not even an option. It was so bad that we knew we had to do something. Therefore I called my dad and Debby, asking if they would take her for the summer so that she could have a time to think about her actions.

Two months later, she came home. I had received the compassionate agape love of God and felt all this tender love for her. I wanted to respect her as a youth, but I so badly just wanted to hold her in my arms. In fourteen years of watching her grow up, I never knew how to love my little girl. I felt like I had lost a lifetime with my children. The compassion I felt for her was bubbling over. For the first time, I could look at her and feel my love for her. It was so exciting to love her this way, but it was too late. Six months later, she moved back out to live with my dad and his wife.

Twenty-one years later, she called me on Boxing Day. She told me that she had never been close to me as a child, that she had nothing in common with me. She was disowning me as her mother. Candy was now thirty-five years old. Up until then, she had been part of my life. We shared birthdays and Christmases. We would visit often, and she would bring the boys to see me. But in the last year, since she disowned me, my heart has been breaking. I don't see my daughter anymore, nor do I see my grandson or the two boys they adopted. It was after my daughter broke all ties with me that I started to tell my story.

Six years after I started attending the Pentecostal Church, Maurice started coming with me. But still he could not find it in his heart to forgive me for the adulterous affair I had committed. Except for a piece of paper that had our marriage license printed on it, our marriage was over. We were two miserable adults living together as husband and wife. The only thing holding us together was the fact that we felt divorce was a sin.

Jamie took sick. He was throwing up green slime. His side hurt so bad that he could only crawl. We tried taking him into the hospital, where our family doctor was on-call. He told us that our child only had the flu. "Take him home and give him an aspirin," he told us. The next day I called the hospital, and again our Doctor was on call. He got miserable with me and told me to not bother him with it.

The next morning, I went down to Jamie's bedroom to check on him. He was not responding to me and his colour did not look right. I called my friend. She helped me take him to the hospital in Ingersoll. The doctor on-call took one look at him and told me he had cancer. He was at the end. All his vital organs were shutting down. Jamie was rushed by ambulance to London's Sick Children's Hospital. They took him right into surgery. I called Maurice at work. He wasted no time getting there. We sat in silence on the floor outside of the OR doors, waiting. I felt such a peace as I sat there. It was not until the surgeon cut in that they knew he only had appendicitis. His appendix had been busted for three days. All his vital organs were full of poison.

During surgery, however, Jamie's heart rate started dropping fast, leading the doctors to discover that he had heart trouble. He came out of the surgery okay, but now we were told that his main coronary artery had stopped growing at birth, so he had no more than a trickle of blood going through his aorta, the artery that sent the blood flowing to his legs. There would have to be more surgery. This surgery was so dangerous that they would not do it until he lost all feelings in his legs. His health condition as it was left him in constant danger of having a severe stroke, but all we could now do was wait. He survived!

It was close to six months later when early one morning Jamie called to me from the bathroom. He could not feel his legs. He was on the floor and could not stand up. I called an ambulance, then called Maurice at work. This new surgery was horrendously dangerous. In order to do the surgery, the doctors had to cut off blood flow to his entire body. There was no blood flowing through his body for six hours. They could not cut the flow from the brain, however. Therefore, donated blood was pumped through his brain. No child had yet come through this surgery walking. Any who had lived through it ended up paralyzed from the neck down. Therefore, his chance of walking again was zero percent, and his chance of living at all was only twenty-five percent.

For six hours, I sat quiet in the room as I waited to hear whether my child was going to live or not. Or whether he would walk again. When the surgeon came out, he was trembling. He looked as pale as a ghost, but something in my spirit that told me that my son was alive. I leaped to my feet. Maurice and I hurried to the Surgeon. I exclaimed, "My baby's alive. He made it through the surgery."

The surgeon told us, "Yes, he made it through the surgery. It will be four more hours before we know whether he's paralyzed."

Our family members who had stayed comforted us and took Maurice and me out for dinner. Later that evening, my husband and I went into the ICU. Jamie was just waking up. We had only just entered when the nurse pulled a tube out of him. He hauled off and kicked her. She was in pain; we could see it in her face. Maurice and I started laughing. We knew now that our boy was going to walk again. That night when my husband and I walked in our house, we threw our arms around each other and started jumping up and down, screaming at the top of our lungs. That was when we both went silent. As we stood and stared each other in the face, we realized that somewhere in those six months we had fallen in love with each other. God could have healed Jamie, but no; instead He healed our marriage.

> The Lord is my shepherd; I shall not want. He makes me to lie down in green pastures; He leads me beside the still waters. He restores my soul; He leads me in the paths of righteousness for His name's sake. Yea, though I walk through the valley of the shadow of death, I will fear no evil; For You are with me; Your rod and Your staff,

they comfort me. You prepare a table before me
in the presence of my enemies; You anoint my
head with oil; My cup runs over. Surely goodness
and mercy shall follow me all the days of my life;
And I will dwell in the house of the Lord forever.
(Psalm 23)

As we waited through Jamie's surgery, not knowing whether
our child would walk again, or if he would even live, we *did* walk
through the valley of death. And His rod and staff *did* comfort
us. That day, a miracle did take place. Last year, Maurice and I
celebrated our twenty-ninth wedding anniversary.

Growing up as a child, I had seen the power of the Devil. But
as a new believer, I was now going to start witnessing the power
of the living God. I had only been attending Hi-Way Church for
two months when I witnessed my sister's healing. No one had
told her that I was attending the Pentecostal Church, yet I was
the first person she went to after she found out that she had breast
cancer. She was living in Goderich, and of course I was living in
Ingersoll, so there were nearly eighty miles between us.

I was walking my kids down the street when Cathy pulled up.
She told me, "Pat, get back to the house. I need to talk to you."
That was when she broke out in tears. I went back with her. She
told me she had breast cancer. My whole body was trembling,
like I was taking a mild convulsion. I was wise enough to know
that this was the power of God. I asked her if she believed that
God could heal her. Between sobs, she nodded her head and said,
"Yes, I believe God can heal me." I laid my hands on her and
immediately started to speak in tongues. It was after I prayed for
her that my tremendous shaking stopped. Later that afternoon,
she called me and said that the lump on her breast had turned to
powder and dropped off. This would be the first of many healings
I would see God perform, on others as well as on myself. Today
Cathy knows Jesus as her personal Lord.

In my early years attending the Pentecostal Church, Sunday nights were my favourite. My Dad had many years before he warned me to stay away from the Pentecostal Church. He told me, "They do strange things. Don't get involved with them. They roll in straw, both men and women together." The Sunday night services had as large a turnout as in the morning. After our pastor preached, he would open the altar. He did this every Sunday night. We would sing hymns from the hymnbook, and Phillis Smith would play the piano. She could make those piano keys dance. Everyone went up. Very few would stay back in the pew. We did not go up to seek God for what we wanted. We went up to worship. The power that fell on these true worshipers was amazing. We were not taking from God; we were giving. No one was concerned about how late it was getting to be, or the time they would go home. They just could not take in enough of this amazing God.

At one of these evening services, the altar was full and there was no standing room left. Our music leader started to sing *Amazing Grace*. Everyone was in one accord as we sang together. All these years, I could not even stand that name—Grace—spoken in my presence, but this night I started to sing. It had been many years since I had cried with tears. I started to cry real tears. My eyeliner was all over my face. I knew then that God's Grace, His beautiful Grace, had saved me. The night with the oil furnace in my mobile home. The night I was nearly raped, wearing the stolen clothing. Then I cried out to God, and He rescued me. It was God's Grace that watched over me, and now I was standing before the One who loved me, even when I was so steeped in sin. He knew me, having loved me in my mother's womb.

It was normal that many would go down under the power of the Holy Ghost. Most Sunday nights, there were more on the floor on their backs than there were standing. It was not unusual for someone to receive the gift of speaking in tongues. This would happen every Sunday night. No one was thinking about

Tim Horton coffee or the other concerns of life; they were in the presence of the King. I never missed a Sunday night service.

I had not yet said very much to my family of what was happening in my life. Later that year, I was attending the first Christmas dinner with my family since I having been saved. Every one of my family members, plus all my in-laws, knew not to say the word Grace in front of me. They were aware of what would happen if anyone said that word. There was one there that was just newly dating my sister, Tammy. No one had warned him. When dinner was fully ready, he called out, "Where's grace?" The room went silent and every eye turned to me. They knew what to expect. I was going to lose my cool. He was going to land face down in a snow bank.

But what happened next, no one was ready for. I sang out with a cheerful tone, "Here I am," and then lowered my head as I lead in saying grace. When I looked up, my mother was crying. Cathy stood there with her mouth wide open. She could not find the words to say as she stared at me. That evening after dinner, I sang *Amazing Grace* for my family. My mother came up beside me and sang along with me. When I finished, there was not a dry eye in the room.

On Christmas Day, my daughter gave me a beautiful grandson. I was so excited about his birth. I was so proud of Candy, and so proud of this little boy. She named him Christian. A girlfriend of mine rejoiced with me. She gave me a gift that for many years to come I would be able to share with him. It was a children's book. She told me that she had gotten it at a Christian bookstore. I took the book home, put it on the book shelf, and left it there. Christian was still very tiny and his mother and Dad, mainly kept him home with them. Therefore, I was waiting for the opportunity to read the story to him.

I kept getting the thought in my head that I should look at the book, but there was always something to be done. I found myself too busy to look at it. Three months had past, and everything was peaceful. Then suddenly, all spiritual chaos broke loose, and this time it was much worse than it had been before. The attacks I had received before would now happen when I was awake. When I tried calling to God for help, the demon pinned my tongue to the back of my mouth, preventing me from calling out. I had never been able to pray in my heart. When I tried to pray in silence, I would get all confused. So calling on Jesus through my thoughts was not going to work. Not only that, but this demon would not let me sleep. I was tormented day and night.

I made an appointment with a Christian counsellor. He had me sit down and take time to think of anything that could have caused this sudden problem to occur. After talking with him, I went home and pulled this book from the bookcase. The cover of the book looked fine. The story was about a grandfather who was a pastor. His grandson came to him for advice. But when I opened the book, I was shocked. Every page had demons on it. They were jumping off of the pages. There was black magic in the book. It amazed me how this book even got into a Christian bookstore.

Since I had become a Christian, I had been avoiding this type of garbage. I took the book out into our garage, where we had a wood burning stove, and burned it. I figured that would be the end of it, but this did not improve my problem. I tried in the name of Jesus to cast demons out, but nothing was working. I went back to the counsellor and asked for help.

This time, preparations were made and a date was set for a spiritual deliverance. My counsellor believed that I was too healthy a Christian to actually have demons inside of me, so he figured the problem was all on the outside. He told me the problem was a demon connected to me. My counsellor told me that something would happen before the date for the deliverance, something that would cause me to feel the need to cancel it. Perhaps it would be a death, sickness, or something else equally serious. But by all means, he told me not to cancel this date.

I went home knowing very well how persistent demons could be, but I also knew how stubborn I could be. One week before the date, I fell and broke my hip. I went by ambulance to the Ingersoll Hospital and from there to London. I would be one week in London, then go back to Ingersoll, where I would be back under the care of my own family doctor. My first night back in Ingersoll was the night set for my deliverance. I had a girlfriend backing me up. Between the two of us, we were trying to figure out how I was going to make it to that deliverance. To this point, I had not sat in a chair any longer than a half-hour.

On my entrance into Ingersoll Hospital, my friend requested that my doctor talk with the two of us. We explained everything to him and went for a long shot, hoping he would sign me out. To our amazement, he did. The lady across from me in the ward owned a taxi business. Not only this, but they had the only wheelchair transit vehicle in town. As soon as she overheard our request, she offered her assistance in getting me to London. Several of the nurses on my ward were Christians. They got me into a wheelchair and snuggled me up warm with blankets. Pretty soon, my friend and I were on our way.

When the demon started to leave, it felt like someone was rolling my wheelchair back and forth. I remembered that the night I led the séance, the very same thing had happened. After the deliverance was over, I asked who was moving the wheelchair. I was told that no one touched it. I knew then that this spirit was the one I had seen on the night of the séance. It had connected itself to me that night. Later that night, as I lay in my hospital bed, in my spirit I was held as a baby in my Heavenly Father's arms. He had me wrapped in a receiving blanket as He rocked me to sleep.

I would spend three more months in the Ingersoll Hospital, and for the next six months after that I would have a time of peace. But after my hip was healed, my problem again started up. This time, along with preventing me from sleeping, the demons became more aggressive. They were physically taking me and shoving me up against the wall. They would yank me across the room and force me to the floor, where they would pin me down. Still I could not pray in my head. I would become disoriented. Trying to cast the demons out of the room on my own was not working. I had the church praying for me daily. That was the only way I could get any sleep. Ninety percent of the time, I did not sleep.

The counsellor told me he had done all he could to help me. I tried two more Christian counsellors. One was helpful to a point, while the other was not at all helpful. The night my daughter and her husband moved to Fergus from London was the only time I felt any comfort. Her husband Frank had unfinished business in London, so he stayed the night there. Candy, myself, and Christian stayed the night in Fergus. Through the late night hours, my daughter became aware of me crying. As always, the spirits were keeping me awake. A person can only go so long without sleep. She took a book, cuddled me in her arms, and read to me. When my little girl read a book, she made it sound like poetry. I was then comforted.

That night, it was like our roles in life had changed. I was the frightened child and Candy gave me comfort. She and my grandson slept that night. I sat all night in the corner of the room, and so it was that when Candy read to me I felt peace just like Saul felt when David played for him (see 1 Samuel 16:23).

I tried sleeping pills, but they did not work. Some Christian friends had suggested reading the Bible through the night. They thought this would cause the spirit to flee, but this did not work, either. It did give me an idea, however. I was not sleeping anyhow, so I started through the night studying books on the power of God. All through the night while my husband slept, I sat at the kitchen table with the Bible, a study book, a notebook, and a pen in my hand. I hoped this would make the spirit flee, which it did not. But I was learning. I was benefiting from it.

I studied one book, then went to the Christian bookstore and picked up another, called *Good Morning, Holy Spirit,* by the author Benny Hinn. I brought it home and proceeded through the night to study it. I had only thought of the Holy Spirit as an *it.* As much as I attended the Pentecostal Church, the pastor had never mentioned that the Holy Spirit could be a personal friend. Neither had anyone else. But according to this book, he could be my friend. I only had to talk to him, so that's what I started doing. In the morning, I would say, "Good morning, Holy Spirit," and at night, "Good night, Holy Spirit." Even though I was not sleeping, I still did this. I was gabbing with the Holy Spirit about everything. I even talked about the weather with Him. He became my best friend. I had suffered now for three years. My burden had only lifted for the short time when my hip was healing.

It was shortly after I finished studying this book that I started to speak in tongues. I started thinking something was up when I had been continually speaking in the Spirit for over six hours. Maurice looked at me strange when he became aware that I had been speaking in tongues for twenty-four hours. He was answering the phone and telling callers I would call back. I spoke in tongues for seventy-two straight hours without breaking.

Then the Holy Spirit started casting spirits out of me. He would ask the spirit its name. The evil spirit would speak through me and say what its name was and its purpose for entering me. Every time the Holy Spirit would cast out a demon, I would throw it up like I was barfing.

I mentioned earlier about the spirit guide, which was one of the spirits that came out. I was having difficulties with sexual thoughts towards my children, plus anyone in general. There were numerous spirits of sexual perversion that came out. Among these were spirits of incest. There were also spirits of witchcraft, some of which said they had been in the family as far back as the 1700s. I had distant relatives on my mother's side who had been burned at the stake. Some of these spirits had entered me at my conception. They confirmed that the Italian man was my father. There were two that had entered when I kneeled at the grave and spoke to the dead. Among the spirits cast out were spirits of caffeine, gluttony, anorexia, nicotine, and alcoholism.

I barfed up three nests. Many that came out called themselves legions. As it took seventy-two hours to pray, so also it took seventy-two hours to cast out all the evil spirits. The Bible warns us to avoid all wickedness. That is not without a purpose. Our Heavenly Father desires to bless us with goodness. If you were to place the palm of your hand on the stove burner while it is hot, you would burn your hand. So it is if you do evil; you will get burnt!

That evening, after the Holy Spirit set me free, I went out to a church function. This was an all-you-can-eat spaghetti dinner. As party favours, there were also Hershey chocolate kisses on the tables. I had something enormous to celebrate, and I had not eaten in six days. I believe I may have gone back for even a third helping of spaghetti.

It is said in the Lord's word,

> When an unclean spirit goes out of a man, he goes through dry places, seeking rest; and finding none, he says, "I will return to my house from which I came." And when he comes, he finds it swept and put in order. Then he goes and takes with him seven other spirits more wicked than himself, and they enter and dwell there; and the last state of that man is worse than the first. (Luke 11:24–26)

I went to bed that night and slept like a baby, but by the next morning I was in greater trouble than I had ever been before. The spirits that had re-entered me were trying to drive me to suicide.

I was a mentally challenged mess. I had my hands clasped on my head as I screamed at the top of my lungs, running through the house like I thought I could get away from the spirits that tormented me. They tried to push me down the steps. If I had stayed in that state, I would have never been released from an insane asylum. I would have been tied down in a straightjacket—and heavily sedated for an infinite time.

Truly, the Spirit of God was the only one who could set me free. With my hands clasped to my head and my fingernails dug into my scalp, I screeched, "Spirit of the living God, help me." It was at that immediate moment, as I called out, that the Holy Spirit started again, speaking in tongues. It would again be three complete days that the Holy Spirit of God would speak in tongues. At the end of those three days, He again cast the spirits out. It was not even close to the number there had been before, but the ones that were there were very wicked. It only took about three hours to cast them all out.

What had I done for this to happen to me? I'd previously had the spirits of caffeine, gluttony, anorexia, nicotine, and alcoholism casted out of me. Therefore, when I went back into the very things that the evil spirits represented, and indulged in them, I opened the door for the spirits to come back in. Not only that, but I had to learn to live a lifestyle of avoiding habitual sins. If I am aware that something is a sin, I must restrain myself from doing it.

The Holy Spirit had me sit down with a paper and pen, taking notes of what I had to avoid in order that these spirits could not again re-enter. Caffeine was an absolute no-no. I also had to learn where the boundary was between healthy eating and gluttony. I had to stick to eating only three meals a day. I could not even eat something as small as a cracker in between my meals. One helping of spaghetti would have been more than enough. Dessert was fine, but I had to consider the size of my portions.

After my full deliverance, the voices in my head stopped and I started sleeping at night. My head was fully cleared, so I could think righteously. There were no more nasty sexual thoughts. Over the past years, I had wanted so earnestly to draw near to my grandson, but out of fear I had avoided him. One afternoon when I was visiting at Candy, shortly after they moved to Fergus, Christian was doing what toddlers enjoy most—running through the apartment in the buff. My dreadful desire to sexually assault him started becoming unbearable. This scared me something bad. I did not have the rights to tell my daughter and her husband how to run their home, so I said nothing. That experience left me terrified to draw near to my grandson. But now that I was delivered, I was fully set free of all these wicked thoughts.

> I will bless the Lord at all times; His praise shall continually be in my mouth. My soul shall make its boast in the Lord; the humble shall hear of it and be glad. Oh, magnify the Lord with me, and let us exalt His name together. I sought the Lord, and He heard me, and delivered me from all my fears. (Psalm 34:1–4)

Blessed be the Lord my God.

# CHAPTER 9

# IT IS POSSIBLE TO FALL AWAY

*M*any Christians believe that once you are born again, you are always born again. This belief greatly bothers me. I believe this is a lie from the devil. It would not be right to write this book and not include this. I do not believe it is impossible to repent of your sins, but if you knowingly sin without repenting, and continue to sin even though the Holy Ghost has tried to prick your conscience, I do believe you can lose your salvation. And it is in my heart that all should be saved. It is possible to fall away, and since we do not know the day or the hour that our Lord will take us home to be with Him in His riches and glory, should we not be prepared every moment for His soon return?

> For it is impossible for those who were once enlightened, and have tasted the heavenly gift, and have become partakers of the Holy Spirit, and have tasted the good word of God and the powers of the age to come, if they fall away, to renew them again to repentance, since they crucify again for themselves the Son of God, and put Him to an open shame. (Hebrews 6:4–6)

I believe many people try to pass over this scripture and avoid it altogether, since they either do not understand it or are frightened by what it says. If according to the Bible the possibility does exist that we could jeopardize our future with our Heavenly Father, would it not be wiser to at least try to live lives worthy of His calling? The only thing I know of that is unconditional with God is His love. He loves every one of us unconditionally, which is what the parable of the wise and foolish virgins means.

> Then the kingdom of heaven shall be likened to ten virgins who took their lamps and went out to meet the bridegroom.
>
> Now five of them were wise, and five were foolish. Those who were foolish took their lamps and took no oil with them, but the wise took oil in their vessels with their lamps. But while the bridegroom was delayed, they all slumbered and slept. And at midnight a cry was heard: "Behold, the bridegroom is coming; go out to meet him!"
>
> Then all those virgins arose and trimmed their lamps. And the foolish said to the wise, "Give us some of your oil, for our lamps are going out." But the wise answered, saying, "No, lest there should not be enough for us and you; but go rather to those who sell, and buy for yourselves." And while they went to buy, the bridegroom came, and those who were ready went in with him to the wedding; and the door was shut.
>
> Afterward the other virgins came also, saying, "Lord, Lord, open to us!" But he answered and said, "Assuredly, I say to you, I do not know you." Watch therefore, for you know neither the day nor the hour in which the Son of Man is coming. (Matthew 25:1–13)

I believe this parable is for those who are saved in Christ. If so, then who are the foolish virgins? They are those who say, "I have accepted Jesus as my Lord. His love is unconditional. A loving God would not send anyone to Hell. It does not matter what I do or say, for I am on my way to Heaven."

I have known some wonderful Christians who stopped serving the Lord for a great number of years, and then successfully came back. The story of the prodigal son (see Luke 15:25–32) is proof that we can stray and then come back to our loving Savour and be welcomed warmly into Heaven. But what if we are active in a sin that we will not repent of when our time is suddenly up? Do you really want to test the scriptures?

# CHAPTER 10

# LETTING GO

*M*y dad held a grievance towards God. He could not find it in his heart to forgive God for the death of Ricky. Therefore, not only was he bitter towards me, but also towards God. His bitterness only got worse as he aged. In his last year, he was dreadfully ill, and this made him cranky to the point that even I found it continually tiresome to visit at his home. Had it not been for his wife Debby, I would have stayed away, but Debby and I had a friendship thicker than blood.

Dad had for the last ten years of his life a heart aneurysm. The doctor had told him that there was no way of knowing when it would burst. Therefore, truly he should have been living every day like it was his last. But he was a rebel, and still a heartless Casanova with all women. Since I had fully dedicated my life to Jesus, I tried endlessly to lead him to the Lord, but I found this impossible. After many years of futile attempts, I quite simply gave up on him. In doing this, I handed him over to Jesus and told Jesus, "Do whatever You need, but just get him into heaven." This resulted in lung cancer, which his doctor found inside the cavity of his lungs. The location of the cancer made it impossible to get at it.

The only thing that could be done was to keep him as comfortable as possible, and wait it out. He did receive chemo for his cancer, but with his other health conditions it took a toll on him. On top of this, he had an artery blockage located in the back of his neck which kept giving him mini strokes.

Another reason I found it hard to go to his home was the fact that he knew my sisters and my brother Jim by their names. When they came to visit him, he recognized them. But when I came in the house, he would ask Debby who this woman was who called him Dad. It was like he was still refusing to acknowledge me as his daughter. He was as cold as ice with me. This hurt me badly.

Later in his life, he became physically abusive towards all women. Debby was continually covering up bruises from the beatings she received from him. He often threatened to hit me, and yet Maurice would take me every week to visit my father. But it was my mother who he would not let me see. My husband liked my dad, but not my mom.

I no longer found myself longing for my father's acceptance. But I was continually struggling to love and forgive him, knowing very well that it was in God's will and desire that I should forgive him. And so I finely gave up on winning his heart over.

As he drew close to the end, Dad got to the point where he had to be hospitalized. He spent most of his last three months in the hospital. I had been in the habit of calling him everyday without ceasing, just to say over the receiver, "I love you, Dad." So when he was hospitalized, I continued to do this. I would leave my message with his nurse to say, "I love you, Dad." I did this to the very day he passed away.

Three days before he died, in December 2000, I went to visit him in the hospital. I had peace that his soul was right with God, which was strange since I knew the type of person he was. My sisters Sherry and Tammy were also there. They were sitting on the hospital bed on both sides of Dad. He was sandwiched in between them. They were close enough that he could lean on them. I knew in my heart that this was goodbye.

I asked if one of them would move, so I could sit next to my dad. Sherry moved and I sat next to him. He asked who it was that called him Dad. I said, "I am Pat." He responded with, "Oh," then leaned over and rested his head on Tammy's shoulder. I knew it was over, and that he had never accepted me. Three days later, he died.

He was alone with Debby when he passed away. After I found out, Maurice took me to the hospital so that I could be with his body. You might find this strange, but my dad always had an odour. You knew he was in the room because you could smell him—not in a bad way; it was a pleasant smell. When I walked into the hospital room, this smell was gone. His body was still lying in the bed. His mouth was wide open, and it was in the shape of a perfect circle.

You could sense his spirit was not there. Although I had been a Christian for many years, and fully aware of life after death, it was like the Spirit of God was making it real to me in a new way. For the first time, I was fully aware that the spirit truly did live on for eternity, and that there truly is a Heaven and hell. I did not feel sad. Instead I felt at peace.

It was only one week later that I had a dream. This would be the first of seven dreams. In this dream, my dad met me by the seashore. He looked young again, like he had when I was a small child. Without any effort, he could leap three stories high. He could also fly. He told me that he loved me and thanked me for praying him into Heaven. He told me that it was my prayers that got him there. He asked me to pray for my siblings, so that they would be in Heaven as well. My father would visit me in my sleep six more times. With every visit, he would shower me with love.

It was two months after his death that my youngest sister told me that he had accepted Christ as his Savior. Two weeks before he died, my dad decided he wanted to go home. I figure he probably thought he could die at home. Nevertheless, right at this time three black men from a church in London came to his home. Rebecca told me that she had witnessed this in their kitchen. One of the men asked Dad if he wanted to ask Jesus to be his Lord. Dad started to cry and said yes. In the presence of these three men, he asked Jesus into his heart. It was immediate that he started to speak in tongues. and then the Spirit of God led him in singing praises to God. Less than a half-hour later, he had to go back to the hospital. He never came back out after that.

I found out six months later that it was not the cancer that killed him. His aneurysm had burst, so you see, my father going to Heaven was truly a miracle. Often I will ask God to pass a message on to my Dad—"Please, dear Father, pass this message: I love you, Dad."

# CHAPTER 11

# IT IS WELL WITH MY SOUL

*W*hen a chance comes your way to share the Gospel, no matter how embarrassing it may be, don't let it pass you by. You don't know how many lives it could change. My sister Tammy called me up one day and asked if I could come to her home and conduct a funeral for their family pet. Their dog had passed away and she had the ashes at home. I agreed to this and went to her home.

There were about twenty people who had come to the funeral. I preached a sermon on the subject of "All Good Dog's Go to Heaven." Then I read the Twenty-Third Psalm. We sang Amazing Grace, and afterward I had as many as who wanted share their special memories of the dog. I asked how many people there were positive without a doubt that if they were to die right then and there, they would go to Heaven. Then I prayed the sinners prayer with all of them. I later found out that two people present had solemnly given their lives to Jesus at that funeral, and they are serving the Lord to this day.

Over the years, I have received some amazing healings. There have been so many that I have only chosen to share the two that I find the most outstanding. One day, I was in a rush and my time was very limited. I had to get out the door to visit my husband.

He had been very ill, and that year he had spent six months in the hospital. I had a broom in my hand and my four-pound Chihuahua was feeling a little like Mommy had been avoiding her. With excitement, she came out to greet me. I did not see her until after I smacked her on the side of her face with the broom handle. Right away, I picked her up to make sure she was okay. She had a lump on the side of her face, and it was as big as her head. She looked like she was in shock. I panicked and started praying, "Dear God, please heal my baby." It was immediate that the lump started to go down as fast as it had come up. My little dog was healed.

As I said, I was born with a mental disability which made it impossible for me to read or write. I could not learn well enough to pass Grade One. I would find the most simple projects so perplexing that I could not even touch them. I did not have the skill to put together anything more complicated than a baby's wooden block puzzle. One afternoon, my husband and I were sitting in my son's living room. There was a two thousand piece puzzle sitting partly finished on his coffee table. A sudden, unexplainable urge came over me to start placing the pieces of the puzzle together. In a matter of thirty seconds, I had placed twenty pieces in their right positions. I did not have a clue what was taking place until suddenly Jamie spoke up, "Mom! What are you doing? That's my puzzle!" That day, I was fully healed of my mental disability. After that, the Lord taught me how to do many things. Today I run my own seamstress business, and I do all my own bookkeeping.

What my mother did to me was the most painful thing I ever had to endure. Although I had been set free of the anger and had many years ago forgiven her, taking Ricky's life in the manner she did was a tremendous blow that left a thick, invisible wall between us. It was so enormous that I could not even come close to chiselling away at it. I could see this wall in my spirit.

After she accepted Jesus as her Lord, she became the most beautiful, precious woman. She was getting up in years, and my fear was that I would never get close to her before she died. If that happened, I knew I would regret not drawing near to her for the rest of my life. Since it was just too great a burden for me to handle, I pleaded with God numerous times to take the wall down. When I had someone to take me, I would visit her in the nursing home. Maurice would not take me, as he did not care for my mother. Our friend Trevor had become a saintly friend to me, however, and in the last few years he made sure I got to see my mom.

It was on one of my last visits with her when I saw in my heart that the wall had finally come down. I was free to draw close to her and love her freely, as I had longed for so many years. I knew she could feel this as well. We were finally set free from all the bitterness. We could rejoice in our love for each other. We clung to each other that day. Leaving her to go home was the most difficult thing I had ever done. I just wanted that moment with my mom to last forever. I could tell by the way she clung to me that she didn't want me to leave, either.

Six months later, my mother went to be with Ricky and Dad. I found peace in letting her go. Did she end up paying for his death? Yes, every day of her life she paid.

As I draw to a conclusion, I remember being hurt so many times. I have shared so many of my deep, dark secrets, but I have also been so greatly blessed. I have prayed that my daughter would have a change of heart. Only a mother could understand how much this hurts, but when it is at the worst, I have learned to count my many blessings and see what God has done.

Just the other day I read "The Ugly Duckling." I have taken the time to look back at where I came from, and the person my child hood made me to be. I also think about what Jesus did for me. I can now look through Jesus' eyes and see the beautiful person I have become—not by my outward appearance, but on the inside, for I have been made new in Christ. So you see, the ugly duckling has turned into a lovely swan.

When peace like a river, attendeth my way,
When sorrows like sea billows roll;
Whatever my lot, Thou hast taught me to say,
It is well, it is well, with my soul.
Though Satan should buffet, though trials should come,
Let this blest assurance control,
That Christ has regarded my helpless estate,
And hath shed His own blood for my soul.[2]

---

[2] Spafford, Horatio. "It Is Well with My Soul," 1873.

Printed in the United States
By Bookmasters